BUT FOR WHOM CHARLIE

Books by S. N. Behrman

Portrait of Max
The Worcester Account
Duveen

Plays

But for Whom Charlie
Lord Pengo
The Cold Wind and the Warm
Fanny
   (*In collaboration with* Joshua Logan)
Jane
   (*Based on the story by* W. Somerset Maugham)
I Know My Love
Dunnigan's Daughter
Jacobowsky and the Colonel
   (*In collaboration with* Franz Werfel)
The Pirate
The Talley Method
No Time for Comedy
Wine of Choice
Amphitryon 38
   (*Adapted from the French of* Jean Giraudoux)
End of Summer
Rain from Heaven
Biography
Brief Moment
Serena Blandish
Meteor
The Second Man

BUT FOR WHOM
CHARLIE

by S. N. BEHRMAN

 Random House • New York

FOR THE ARTISTS OF THE REPERTORY THEATER
OF LINCOLN CENTER

BUT FOR WHOM CHARLIE *was first presented by the Repertory Theater of Lincoln Center for the Performing Arts at the ANTA Theatre, New York City, on March 12, 1964, with the following cast:*

(In order of appearance)

NAOMI SAUNDERS	Patricia Roe
SEYMOUR ROSENTHAL	Jason Robards, Jr.
ANNA	Diane Shalet
CHARLES TANEY	Ralph Meeker
FAITH PROSPER	Faye Dunaway
WILLARD PROSPER	Clinton Kimbrough
GILIAN PROSPER	Salome Jens
BROCK DUNNAWAY	David Wayne
HARRY LORCH	Michael Strong
SHEILA MALONEY	Barbara Loden

Directed by Elia Kazan

Production and lighting by Jo Mielziner

Music arranged by David Amram

Production stage managers: Robert Downing
Frederic de Wilde

The entire action of the play takes place in the headquarters of the Seymour Rosenthal Foundation, in the East Sixties, in New York City.

The time is now.

Act One

ACT I

Scene: The combination office–living room of CHARLES
TANEY'S *apartment on the second floor of a charming house
in the East Sixties. The house is the headquarters of the
Seymour Rosenthal Foundation. The first two floors are
occupied by* CHARLES TANEY, *the Director of the Foundation; the three upper floors by* SEYMOUR ROSENTHAL. *At
right is a door to a staircase leading up to* ROSENTHAL'S
quarters. Visible above is one of ROSENTHAL'S *rooms, a
study; in it we see a table with a telephone on it, a chair
with a goose-necked lamp leaning over it, one of his pictures on a wall, and a door leading to another room. The
impression given by* SEYMOUR'S *room, in contrast with the
office–living room below, is one of austerity.*

CHARLIE'S *office–living room is very cozy and comfortable
—full of avant-garde pictures, tables loaded with manuscripts, galleys, submissions for consideration.*

Time: It is about six o'clock on an April afternoon.

At Rise: NAOMI SAUNDERS, *secretary to the Foundation,
is tidying up the overburdened table, preparatory to depart-
ing, as her working day is over.* MISS SAUNDERS *is thirty,
attractive and hep. She is slick; there are no flies on* MISS
SAUNDERS. *Just as she is leaving, with a sigh of relief,*
SEYMOUR ROSENTHAL *wanders in. He gives the impression
of having come from no place in particular and to be not
quite certain of where he is going. He carries a bulging
brief case.* SEYMOUR *is about thirty-five, dark, slim, gentle,
beginning to get bald. His manner is hesitating; he is near-
sighted and has an anxious, somewhat pained, inquiring
look. There is the faintest suggestion of a stammer in his*

speech; you cannot quite tell whether it is a stammer or whether he is merely inarticulate. He starts sentences and doesn't finish them, as if he were assailed midway by doubts about the validity of what he is saying. MISS SAUNDERS, *who is just about to leave, tries to suppress the annoyance she feels at running into* SEYMOUR *at just this moment.*

MISS SAUNDERS   Oh, good evening, Mr. Rosenthal.

SEYMOUR   Oh, Miss Saunders. How are you?

MISS SAUNDERS   Just leaving . . .

SEYMOUR   Is Mr. Taney about?

MISS SAUNDERS   (*Who knows perfectly well*) I really don't know. You know Mr. Taney! He's here and then he's not here. (*During this,* SEYMOUR *has gone to the manuscript-piled table and begun looking through the scripts*) Anything I can do for you, Mr. Rosenthal?

SEYMOUR   Those poems—by that Irish girl . . . I seem to have . . . But don't you bother, Miss Saunders . . . you're always working overtime as it is . . .

MISS SAUNDERS   Sheila Maloney's?

SEYMOUR   Yes. I know I took them . . . Has Mr. Taney read them?

MISS SAUNDERS   (*With contempt for* SHEILA MALONEY) I think he tried!

SEYMOUR   She's difficult . . . special vocabulary . . . but I think she's worth . . .
      (*By this time his search is becoming a little frantic*)

BUT FOR WHOM CHARLIE

MISS SAUNDERS (*Her contempt transferring itself subtly to* SEYMOUR) Have you tried your brief case? Do you mind? (*She opens his brief case, which* SEYMOUR *has left on a chair, riffles through it expertly and extracts a manuscript*) Here they are! (*Reads from first page*) Poems—Sheila Maloney.

SEYMOUR (*Relieved and abashed*) Oh, thank you, Miss Saunders. You are really very . . . and I am . . .

MISS SAUNDERS (*With irony*) You have so much on your mind, Mr. Rosenthal! Anything else?

SEYMOUR Oh, no. Thank you very much, Miss Saunders.

MISS SAUNDERS Not at all. Good night.

SEYMOUR (*Scribbles on a pad on the table*) Good night, Miss Saunders. I'll just leave a note for Mr. Taney—to call me—when he comes in—

(MISS SAUNDERS *goes.* SEYMOUR *props the note up against the telephone so it will be visible, takes* SHEILA MALONEY's *poems, stuffs them back into his brief case and walks slowly up the stairs. We see him go into his room, put his brief case on the table beside the chair under the goose-neck lamp, light the lamp, take out the poems again, put on reading glasses, which he takes from the table, and start reading. The telephone rings downstairs.* ANNA, *a wispy, fast-moving, vitally energetic maid in her early forties, famous in* CHARLIE's *circle for her cooking and for her asperities, comes almost running in, as is her habit, to answer the telephone*)

ANNA (*On the telephone*) I'm sorry Mr. Taney's not in . . . Yes, this is Anna—who're you? . . . Oh, Doctor

5

Greer . . . oh well, if it's you, Doctor Greer, I guess I can tell *you*—Mr. Taney *is* in but he asked me not to disturb him . . . I *can't* disturb him if you know what I mean . . . (ANNA *giggles hysterically*) Oh well, if he called you I guess he'll . . . (*At this point* CHARLES TANEY *comes in.* CHARLES *is thirty-five, very good-looking, smartly dressed, radiant with health, bounding vitality and delight in living*) Oh, just a minute . . . here he is now . . . (*To* CHARLIE) It's Doctor Greer . . .

CHARLIE   Oh sure . . .
        (*She hands over receiver*)

CHARLIE (*On the phone*)   Hello Alvin . . . ?

ANNA (*As she goes*)   I'd like to speak to you about something, Mr. Taney, when you get through . . .

CHARLIE (*Smiles at her*)   Sure, pet. I'll only be a minute . . . (ANNA *goes out.* CHARLIE *resumes on the telephone*) Oh, well enough, learned Doctor . . . Oh, just at the minute . . . a bit down, but I'll get over that . . . Oh, you know . . . (*His gaiety belies it*) Post coitum melancholia . . . don't you know I majored in classics at Yale? . . . I was going to call you, as a matter of fact . . . How was the big meeting with Rosenthal? I'm agog to know . . . What? He didn't . . . Well, the cowardly . . . I'm not surprised actually . . . even back at Yale he was always making dates with psychoanalysts and breaking them at the last minute . . . gets into a kind of funk about it . . . or maybe, having made the date, he feels better . . . Anyway, Alvin, don't worry, I'll get him to you . . . hell, *I* go to you and I'm better adjusted than you are . . . as Seymour is my lord and master I want him to be in good mental health . . . but, Alvin, an awful thought just hit me . . . if Seymour *were* in good mental health maybe he'd give up this noble altruistic Foundation and I'd be out of a job . . . can I *afford* to get him to you? What? . . . I want you to make him independent—but not of me. (*Evidently Doctor Greer is laughing. So is* CHARLIE) O.K., Alvin. Leave it to me. (*Looks at the pad on the desk*) Oh, sure. Four-thirty Friday—I'll be there—*I'm* in no funk about seeing you, Alvin—in fact, it gives me a sense of superiority— I know so much more about life than you do. Okey-doke. (*He hangs up. The laughs he has gotten from his doctor have put him in good humor. He lights a cigarette and goes to the door through which he has come out, opens it a little, then he calls*) Faith? O.K.?

FAITH'S VOICE   O.K. Be out in a minute.

CHARLIE   I'll have a martini for you. (*He closes door, goes to bar and starts mixing drinks. While he is doing this* ANNA *comes back*) Anna, my precious, what's on your mind?

ANNA   Plenty.

CHARLIE (*Concerned—she is so grim*)   What is it, Anna?

ANNA (*Bluntly*)   I'm quitting.
(CHARLIE *is aghast. This is devastating. He puts down the cocktail mixer, walks to her*)

CHARLIE   You're not serious!

ANNA   Got to!

CHARLIE   But, Anna! Is anything wrong? I adore you. I always thought you were happy here. Aren't you?

7

ANNA I'm happy enough with you, but my doctor ain't.

CHARLIE What?

ANNA Yes. I've been going for four years. And he says you're not right for me. He says on account of you and the way you live and all that, I've got sexual inferiority.

CHARLIE I never heard of anything so absurd.

ANNA (*With finality*) Doctor's orders.

CHARLIE Change your doctor.

ANNA My doctor's God to me.

CHARLIE (*Pitifully*) You don't know what you're doing to me, Anna. I just can't imagine life without you. My popularity depends entirely on you. Why do my friends love me? Because they love your cooking. Anna—I implore you—don't desert me.

ANNA (*With a certain hostility*) Oh, you'll manage. Nothing'll stop *you!*

CHARLIE (*Sinks to his knees before her, his palms together in supplication*) Anna—I beg you . . .
    (FAITH *comes in from the bedroom. She is a lovely girl of twenty-four*)

FAITH Hello, Anna. Charlie making love to you?

ANNA (*Throws her a look of aversion*) Not me!

CHARLIE Anna, I beg you! Faith begs you!

ANNA (*Curtly*) Sorry. Doctor's orders. The fifteenth I leave. I'll be glad to break anybody in.
    (*She starts out.* CHARLIE *stands up*)

8

CHARLIE (*Desperate*) Anna! Wait a minute.

ANNA (*Doggedly*) No use. I've got another job!

CHARLIE (*Aghast—this is the death knell*) You have?

ANNA My next boss is going to be a lady!
(*She goes out*)

CHARLIE (*Limp*) I'll be God damned! These psycho-analysts are a menace!

FAITH What have they got to do with it?

CHARLIE Her psychoanalyst told her I'm not right for her.

FAITH (*Laughs*) Really?

CHARLIE I'm glad you think it's funny. I'm bruised. And you think it's funny!

FAITH I certainly do. Where's that martini?
(CHARLIE *returns to the bar*)

CHARLIE In ten years—in ten years—I haven't had a sec-retary who hasn't asked if she can come in late two mornings a week because she has to go to her analyst. God damn it, why do people take their egos so seriously?
(*He gives* FAITH *her drink, goes back to his own*)

FAITH People are lonely. They want reassurance—they . . . (*Struck by an idea*) Can it be that poor Anna is in love with you and can't stand the procession of girls that troop in and out of here—of which I am one?

CHARLIE How idiotic can you get!

FAITH You'd be surprised!

9

CHARLIE (*His gaiety returning*) I don't believe in testing people for loyalty—or for anything else—still it will be interesting to see how many people will drop me—once Anna's gone.

(*He catches sight of* SEYMOUR's *note, glances at it, tosses it back on the table. A moment.* FAITH *gathers her strength to make a request*)

FAITH I asked my brother to pick me up here—do you mind?

CHARLIE Not at all. Why should I mind? I like Willard. How's he getting along?

FAITH I'm desperate about him.

CHARLIE I'm sorry to hear that.

FAITH He's got that wretched part-time job in the book store. Between us we have three children to support— my dead brother's children—*and* their mother. That walk-on I've got in Father's play doesn't pay much—

CHARLIE I'll be glad to help—to tide Willard over—

FAITH I know how kind and generous you are. But it isn't a question of a loan. No matter what you lent him it'd be only a stopgap. But you could do something that really would help him. That would encourage him, give him a new lease on life. A grant. A grant from the Seymour Rosenthal Foundation.

CHARLIE Well—a grant for what—for what project?

FAITH (*Passionately*) It isn't just because he's my brother. I wouldn't ask you if he didn't deserve it. But Willard's a first-rate scholar. Even Father was proud of him.

CHARLIE What project?

FAITH Willard's writing a biography of Chamfort.

CHARLIE Who he?

FAITH He was a figure of some prominence in the French Revolution.

CHARLIE Just what we need!

FAITH Isn't the purpose of Seymour's foundation to publish books that no one else will publish?

CHARLIE (*Gently*) Yes, ostensibly, but it would help if the book had some other qualifications.

FAITH I've seen the part that Will's done and it's fascinating.

CHARLIE Why doesn't he finish it?

FAITH By the time he gets through wrapping bundles in the book shop, he's too tired and discouraged to . . .

CHARLIE He had a teaching job at NYU, didn't he? Why did he give that up?

FAITH I guess you know that too!

CHARLIE (*Gently*) Has he tried Alcoholics Anonymous?

FAITH (*In passionate defense*) Is it any wonder he drinks? It's a wonder he's alive!

CHARLIE You're his sister. You've been through about the same as Willard and yet you're alive. Very much alive.

FAITH I insist on living! I won't die. It would give *her* too much satisfaction.

CHARLIE You're wrong about Gilian. Can you imagine what it was to be *married* to your father?

FAITH I adore you, Charlie. But there's one thing about you that crucifies me—that you like Gilian—that you see Gilian.

CHARLIE You're unfair to Gilian.

FAITH I get the feeling sometimes—

CHARLIE Yes?

FAITH That you'll end up with Gilian—that you mean to marry Gilian.

CHARLIE Gilian, you know, has a mind of her own—a very calculating one. I assure you—I'd be no match for Gilian.

FAITH When Willard was a little boy, at school, his friends would ask why his famous father never came to see him, and Willard had to lie to cover up. To all the litters of children Father left by various wives, he was invisible. When that play came out—telling what poor Dad had had to suffer from his parents and what a vampire Mother was—Willard said—he was seven years old then and he adored Mother—he said: "When I grow up I'll kill my father." That was his first articulate ambition!

CHARLIE Why do you blame all that on Gilian?

FAITH My mother, who saw Father through his years of struggle, died in poverty. Gilian came in for the kill. She sits in the lap of luxury. She has everything. (*A silence*) They should be sterilized, all of them . . .

CHARLIE Who?

FAITH (*With irony*) These men of genius—they should be sterilized so they can't have children.

CHARLIE (*Flippantly*) Difficult to do that, Faith. Violation of the democratic process!

FAITH Don't make fun of me, Charlie!

CHARLIE Have another martini, darling. You're overwrought! (*He gives her another drink. She calms down a bit*) With all that you can say against your father, think of the magnificent works he left . . .

FAITH I wish he hadn't left *us*!

CHARLIE If not for what they do—the artists—life wouldn't be worth living. You'll admit that, won't you?

FAITH If you happen to be their children the price of those masterpieces comes too high! (*She picks up one of her father's books from the table*) "To my dear Charlie, but for whom . . ." (*She drops the book*) I know this book is a masterpiece but I loathe the sight of it. (*Upstairs we see* SEYMOUR, *lost in a dream of meditation over* SHEILA MALONEY's *verses. He lets the manuscript drop into his lap. His hand, almost unconsciously, moves to the button on the table beside him and presses it. We hear the buzz in* CHARLIE's *room.* CHARLIE *walks to answer it*)

13

CHARLIE (*On the telephone*) Seymour, my delinquent boy, how are you?

SEYMOUR Oh, Charlie . . . I left you a note to call me when you got in . . .

CHARLIE Did you? Where is it?

SEYMOUR Oh—it doesn't matter . . . I thought—if you're not busy I'd like . . . I'd just like . . .

CHARLIE What's on your mind?

SEYMOUR These poems . . . Sheila Maloney's . . . the more I read her . . .

CHARLIE (*Incredulous*) Are you *reading* her? How?

SEYMOUR Well, yes, she's difficult . . . but there is . . . she has . . . well, tremendous passion there . . . purity of feeling . . . I can't . . . except I find it very moving . . . she reminds me . . . she makes me think of Simone Weill . . .

CHARLIE (*Winks at* FAITH, *who is listening attentively*) Why don't we publish Simone Weil?

SEYMOUR (*Dead serious*) Well, I'm afraid she's dead and we can do nothing for her. But Miss Maloney . . . well, she's alive.

CHARLIE Why does she break out so much in Italian and Spanish?

SEYMOUR They're the saints. She is absorbed in sainthood. She is a Catholic, I suppose.

14

CHARLIE (*Knowing he never will*) Well, I'll have another go at Sheila. But I've got something more immediate to talk to you about, my beamish boy.

SEYMOUR (*Shrinking from the admonition*) What about?

CHARLIE Doctor Greer called. He says you broke your appointment with him . . . that was naughty of you . . . it took some doing to get you that appointment . . . he's a very busy man, you know.

SEYMOUR I just . . . I don't know . . . at the last minute I just . . .

CHARLIE I know the feeling though I never had it . . . I never care what Alvin asks me . . . I don't even mind if I tell him the truth . . . (*He laughs*) Faith Prosper's with me . . . like to come down? She wants very much to meet you.

SEYMOUR (*Panicked*) Oh, thank you very much . . . but not just this minute . . . I haven't finished . . . I haven't quite finished . . .

CHARLIE Okay. Stick with Sheila and the saints. I'll call you later.

SEYMOUR Please. Please do. I'm not going out.
(*He hangs up. Picks up the manuscript again. Sits a moment. Then he goes into the other room where, presumably, he tries to resolve the emotions induced by* SHEILA *by playing Bach. Intermittently, during the following scenes, we hear Bach's* Fantasia *and* Fugue. *By this time* FAITH, *having finished her martini, is in better spirits*)

15

CHARLIE   Sweet guy—Seymour—but no guts. Can you imagine—afraid to go to an analyst!

FAITH   Why are you so anxious for him to go?

CHARLIE   Because he needs it. He lacks self-confidence.

FAITH   You *are* a darling. No wonder everybody loves you.

CHARLIE   He's so naïve—Seymour. He *does* amuse me with his intensely serious ethical considerations.

FAITH   Everything is funny to you, Charlie. That's what people love about you. Including yours truly.

CHARLIE   Do you know why everything is funny to me, darling? Because everything *is* funny.

FAITH   Perhaps you don't feel anything very much?

CHARLIE   (*Lightly, just saying the easy thing*)   You can't say that. You know how I feel about *you*, for instance.

FAITH   That's precisely what I don't know!

CHARLIE   Good! That'll stimulate you!

FAITH   (*A moment*)   By the way, Charlie—

CHARLIE   What's by the way?

FAITH   I've had an offer of marriage.

CHARLIE   Have you? Anyone I know?

FAITH   Not remotely.

CHARLIE   Then he can't be eligible!
          (FAITH *laughs*)

FAITH   You're a terrible snob, I'm afraid.

16

CHARLIE Who is he?

FAITH He's a bassoonist.

CHARLIE Where does he bassoon?

FAITH He is a non-playing bassoonist.

CHARLIE *That* makes the outlook brighter.

FAITH He's in the orchestra in the play I'm in.

CHARLIE But I don't remember any music in your father's play.

FAITH There isn't. The union insists he sit there every night with four other non-players. He's a featherbedder.

CHARLIE (*Murmurs*) Aren't we all? But you'd better move cautiously, darling—about marrying him I mean—he may play at home when the union isn't looking.

FAITH I'm very taken with him. He's very endearing. I have a feeling if he knew about us—about me and my family, I mean—he'd be scared to death to get involved with me. He's very respectable.

CHARLIE You mean that you are concealing from him the awful intelligence that your father was a Nobel Prize winner?

FAITH Oh, I think he must know that. It doesn't impress him at all.

CHARLIE Isn't he a reader?

FAITH Just Bach cantatas and the racing forms.

17

CHARLIE (*Lightly*) Are you having an affair with him? (*She laughs*) Is the idea funny to you?

FAITH He hasn't even kissed me yet. I know he wants to, but he doesn't dare. You see, darling, he's *romantic* about me. Willard says to grab him. Get as far away as you can, he says, from that literary crowd. When they're written out—as Father got to be—they revenge themselves on everyone around them. They murder right and left just to prove to themselves that they're not dead.

CHARLIE Are there no alternatives but bassoonists?

FAITH I'm not really thinking seriously of marrying my featherbedder. I only told you about it . . .

CHARLIE Well?

FAITH To see if it might produce a counter-offer.

CHARLIE I do adore you, darling.

FAITH (*Wryly*) I know you do. Why not?

CHARLIE I don't know anyone more enchanting.

FAITH What I really want from you, Charlie, is not a wedding ring—though God knows that would be welcome because I love to be with you—but what I really want—and I want it terribly—is this grant for my brother.

CHARLIE (*With a weary sigh, points to the heaped-up pile of manuscripts and galleys on his table*) Requests. Works in progress. Manuscripts. Galleys. Projects. Novels. Poems. Works on philosophy, on cultural history, biographies, Ph.D. theses, ambitions to blossom into books. The yearnings of mid-Western provincials longing to spend their days and nights in the libraries of Europe. I have to read all those. I have to pass on all those.

FAITH (*Looks at the pile—with commiseration*) It must be terrible to have such power.

CHARLIE It's worse than terrible. It's boring.

FAITH Think of the good you can do. Think of the help you can give.

CHARLIE All because Seymour's father was a film tycoon whose sins poor Seymour wants to expiate.

FAITH Willard's first-rate. His book will be first-rate. If I weren't sure of it, I wouldn't ask you.

CHARLIE I'll do what I can for Willard. I'll try.

FAITH Please! Please! It's the only thing I'll ever ask of you.

CHARLIE I'm not sole judge, you know. There's a board.

FAITH Let the board read what Willard's already written . . . *you* read it.

CHARLIE I'll take your word for it . . .! But there are other considerations, you know. I'd better be frank. I'll be up against it with the board, I'm afraid, recommending an alcoholic. Willard wants to go abroad, doesn't he? Well, what assurance can I give that he won't drink himself to death there as his father did?

19

FAITH   Willard's been on the wagon for three months. And with the lift this will give him . . . I stake my life on it, Charlie. You know I wouldn't say it if I didn't—

CHARLIE (*Kindly*)   I know. I do know. Leave it to me, darling. If it can be done—I'll do it. Tell him to send me his manuscript . . . what there is of it—
(ANNA *comes in. At the same moment the telephone rings*)

ANNA (*To* FAITH)   A gentleman to see you, miss.

CHARLIE (*To* ANNA)   Show him up, Anna.
(ANNA *goes.* CHARLIE *goes to answer the telephone*)

CHARLIE (*On the telephone*)   Oh, hello . . . just a minute, darling . . . I'll take it on the other phone . . . (*He leaves the phone. To* FAITH) I'd better take this in the other room . . .

FAITH (*Eaten with jealousy*)   Not Gilian, by any chance?

CHARLIE   As it happens, it *is* Gilian. (*Starts for the door*) I'll see Willard before he goes . . .

FAITH   I can tell him then—that you'll try?

CHARLIE   You certainly can . . .
(CHARLIE *goes out.* ANNA *shows in* WILLARD. WILLARD *is four years older than* FAITH—*twenty-eight. He is tall, gaunt, with a keen eye, and very attractive in a saturnine way*)

FAITH (*Very excited*)   Hello, Will! Oh, Will! I think I have good news.
(WILLARD *looks around the room; he has a hawk-eye. He takes everything in*)

WILLARD   Perfect!

FAITH   Charlie went in to take a call. He'll be in in a minute.

WILLARD *(Looks at the pictures)* Very progressive! *(His eyes leave the pictures and again take in the room)* It's almost too abrupt for me, you know.

FAITH   What is?

WILLARD   The sudden transition—from the lower depths to the upper depths. *(He looks at her)* But you seem to move naturally on this exalted level.

FAITH   Why are you so bitter with me?

WILLARD   I was only remarking—that for me the transition is abrupt—but give me time—I'll get acclimatized.

FAITH   I think that Charlie will get you that grant.

WILLARD *(Goes to the table, picks up a "project," looks at the heading—reads)* "Studies in the Coin Nomenclature of Etruscan Art." Now who—I ask you, who—could pass on this fascinating subject more acutely than Charles Taney? I saw just now—in my favorite column in my favorite newspaper—that Mr. Taney was at the Stork Club last night with our stepmother. Does he go into this, do you suppose *(He weighs the "project" in his hand)* . . . the nomenclature of Etruscan coins, with the headwaiter at the Stork?

FAITH   Well, there's a board—a board of experts.

WILLARD *(Picks up his father's novel, opens it to the dedication page, stares at it—holds it away from him as if he couldn't trust his eyes, then holds it close again and reads)* "For Charlie . . . 'Since my dear soul was mistress of her choice, and could of men distinguish, her election hath sealed thee for herself; for thou hast been as one, in suffering all, that suffers nothing.'" Now, surely Father was drunk when he wrote that. He always spouted Shakespeare when he was drunk.

FAITH *(Impatient)* Oh, let's get away from Father for once!

WILLARD *(Still staring at the inscription)* But does Mr. Taney suffer? I am interested that he suffers. Do you do anything to alleviate his suffering?

FAITH Charlie's very nice. He's a dear.

WILLARD I doubt both allegations.

FAITH He's just promised me—he'll do anything he can to get you that grant. I know he will.

WILLARD Dear sister. Nothing good will come to us from Charles Taney.

FAITH *(Exasperated)* Why do you say that? You hardly know him.

WILLARD *(Still looking around at* CHARLIE's *pictures)* Perfect. In fact, it's too good to be true!

FAITH *(Scared)* Willard! You haven't been drinking!

WILLARD Can't you tell? There are two lucidities. The higher one—the lucidity of alcohol—and the grimmer one—the lucidity of sobriety. Can't you tell?

FAITH (*Relieved*) Thank God—for a moment I was worried.

(*From upstairs we hear Bach played on the piano*)

WILLARD Who in this house plays Bach?

FAITH Mr. Rosenthal, I guess. He lives upstairs.

WILLARD (*Stands behind the table heaped with projects*) Doesn't it amuse you? It does me.

FAITH What?

WILLARD That of all the people to whom Seymour Rosenthal might have given this marvelous and highly lucrative job—the artists, the scholars, the people who really care about such things—that he picked the headwaiter at the Stork Club.

FAITH (*Scared again*) You *are* drunk! I never can tell with you.

WILLARD I couldn't have said that if I were drunk. It's a different order of lucidity.

FAITH If only, Will, you'd give up drinking!

WILLARD (*Mildly*) I don't ask you to give up sex.

FAITH (*Defiantly*) I love Charlie.

WILLARD I had a most amusing time last night with your bassoonist. Since he couldn't find you, he latched on to me. Have you ever been to his flat?

FAITH (*Curtly*) No.

WILLARD You should go. He has two pianos. We fumbled through Beethoven quartets till all hours. He gave me

23

a temperance lecture. You would have approved. To him I am paradoxical. He cannot understand a simultaneous passion for Beethoven quartets and Scotch whiskey. It throws him.

FAITH I hate you in this mood. I almost wish you *were* drunk.

WILLARD Don't worry. You'll get your wish!

FAITH When you're drunk you never want to wound me.

WILLARD (*Really contrite—with tenderness*) Nor do I now, darling. Nor do I ever. It's true I don't like the idea of you and Charlie, but then there's so much in the world—practically everything, in fact—that I don't like. I don't, for instance, like the idea of myself and myself. My beloved Faith, my dear sister, what is to become of us?

FAITH (*Stoutly*) I'll be all right. And if you get this grant—which I believe you will—*you'll* be all right. That's a wonderful book. The subject suits you. It'll turn out. I know it will.
        (*A pause*)

WILLARD I stand in the street . . . cold sober I stand in the street . . .

FAITH What?

WILLARD I see people hurrying by on the street. They are busy, absorbed, hurrying to an objective. I want to join them. But their lives are full. Seemingly full. No vacancies. I stand at the docks and watch cargoes being loaded. There are immense activities; assembly lines spawn prod-

ucts, people buy and sell, Presidents give press conferences, the world is busy. But I am not in the world.
How can I get into the world? Get me a ticket to the
world.

FAITH (*She is affected*) Charlie will give you a ticket.

WILLARD Somehow, darling—I don't know why it is—but
somewhere I feel that a ticket issued me by Charlie
will be refused at the gate.
      (CHARLIE *comes back, full of beans. He goes to*
WILLARD, *gives him his hand*)

CHARLIE Delighted to see you. How are you?

WILLARD The goose hangs high!

CHARLIE (*Makes a gesture toward the bar*) Drink?
      (*Too late to see* FAITH *shaking her head violently
at him*)

WILLARD No, thank you—I'm on the wagon.
      (FAITH *sighs with relief—it was a near thing*)

CHARLIE Well—Faith's been telling me about your project, what's his name?

FAITH Chamfort.

CHARLIE I've never heard of him. That's a good sign,
isn't it? I mean—I'm reasonably educated—I flunked out
at Yale and surely you can't do better than that—and if,
with that impressive background of erudition, I haven't
heard of Chamfort, there must be something wrong. I
mean, not wrong with Chamfort, but with me. I'd love
to read what you've written and then I can talk to you
as one Chamfort man to another.

WILLARD If you become interested I'll turn the project over to you and you can finish it. I'll take over your job and, if I like the way you've finished Chamfort, I'll give *you* a grant.

CHARLIE (*Delighted—turns to* FAITH) Say, Faith! You didn't tell me your brother was amusing. She always tells me what a scholar you are! She makes you sound grim. Come up for dinner. (*Remembers*) Oh, but I forgot. I can't invite you for dinner because I haven't got a cook. Have you told him, Faith, the calamity that befell me?

FAITH (*Smiles, delighted things are going so well*) Not yet, I will.
   (*The Bach stops. The buzzer on* CHARLIE's *desk sounds.* CHARLIE *takes it*)

CHARLIE (*On the telephone*) Yes, Seymour? . . . No, I'm not . . . Miss Prosper's still here and her brother Willard . . . As a matter of fact, Mr. Prosper has a project about which I'm very anxious to talk to you. Be right up.

FAITH (*Swimming in gratitude*) You're a darling!

CHARLIE That's what we're here for—to be darlings. When do I see you, Faith?

FAITH When do you want?

CHARLIE I'll call you in the morning.

FAITH Do.

CHARLIE (*Starts to go*) 'Bye, Willard. Awfully nice to see you.

WILLARD Thank you. Same here.

CHARLIE (*Stops on his way out*) By the way—perhaps I'd better warn you . . .

FAITH Yes?

CHARLIE Gilian's coming. She's having dinner here.

FAITH We'll clear out in time.

CHARLIE (*Just as he's going—to* WILLARD) What's that feller's name again? The feller you're writing about?

WILLARD Chamfort.

CHARLIE (*Memorizing it as he goes upstairs*) Chamfort. Chamfort.

FAITH (*The moment* CHARLIE *is gone*) There! Aren't you encouraged? I'm terribly encouraged. You handled your end very well!

WILLARD That, I believe, is what is called small talk. It was hardly visible.

FAITH What time is it?

WILLARD I pawned my watch. Find I don't need one.

FAITH Well, I've got to be getting to the theatre. We'll have a bite somewhere.

WILLARD Fine.

FAITH I'll just get my coat. Won't be a minute.
    (*She runs to the bedroom.* WILLARD *looks around the room again. Sees the bar. He makes for it. He pours himself a stiff one and swallows it. He pours*

27

*himself another and holds it. He stands at the bar,
talking to himself)*

WILLARD *(Aloud)* Commitment. Involvement. Act.
*(FAITH comes back. She looks at him. She sees what
has happened. She is devastated)*

FAITH Will! Will! *(She runs to him, takes the glass he
holds away from him)* Just now, Willard! When things
are looking up! Just now!

WILLARD Lucidity on a high level. Commitment. Involvement.

FAITH *(In despair)* Just this minute! Did you have to?
*(ANNA comes in. She carries a huge bouquet of
flowers. She puts them in a vase—and the accom-
panying card beside it. She does this as if the task
were distasteful to her and walks out without a
word to FAITH)*

WILLARD *(To FAITH who is looking down at the card that
came with the flowers)* He has admirers, your boy
friend! *(FAITH says nothing)* Are they from the lady of
the Stork, our dear stepmother?
*(Compulsively he goes to the table, picks up the
envelope)*

FAITH Don't do that! *(Nevertheless, he takes out the
card)* They *are* from her. I know her handwriting.
*(WILLARD has opened the envelope, reads the mes-
sage. He laughs. FAITH takes the card and without
reading it, puts it back into its envelope beside the
vase)*

28

WILLARD   She writes funny messages, Gilian—I'll say that.

FAITH   I don't mind hating Gilian. I'm used to that. What I don't like is being jealous of her.

WILLARD   It's very funny. They possess the earth. It's very funny.

FAITH (*In a subdued voice*)   I'll be late for the theatre. Come, Will.

WILLARD (*Mumbling to himself*)   Even if life is meaningless, you must *do* something.

FAITH (*Desperate—her voice rises*)   Will, please! I'm trying to keep up. What do you want to do to me? You scare me!

WILLARD (*Looks at her with deep tenderness, with compassion*)   I scare you! How can *I* scare you? I love you. You're the only thing in the world I love. Out of all the grimy past—

FAITH (*Passionately*)   We've got to stop eternally souping ourselves in the past. It's dead. Let it stay dead.

WILLARD   You're wrong. The past is not dead. It's the only thing that's alive. We're the sum of it.

FAITH (*Desperately*)   There must be some way of getting away from it!

WILLARD   There isn't. You can get away from the present —through drink or sex—but not from the past.

FAITH (*Moves to the street door*)   Take me to the theatre.

WILLARD   All right. Can you sneak me in? I haven't seen it since I was a little boy—the first production. It was a failure then, and now it's a tremendous hit. Royalties for the glamorous widow. (*Gestures toward the flowers*) Flowers for the glamorous Foundation head. Will you sneak me in? I'll stand at the back.

FAITH   If you want to. But why?

WILLARD   I want to see how mean my grandparents were to our poor, brow-beaten Daddy. Whatever he went through he made us go through twice as much. No inheritance tax on *that* legacy. It's so touching. I want to weep for his sufferings. I want to . . .
    (GILLIAN *comes in. She is radiantly lovely. About forty. She walks through life secure in her beauty*)

GILIAN   Oh, I'm sorry . . .

FAITH   We're just leaving . . .

GILIAN   I'm Gilian. I've asked Charlie so many times to let me meet you. But he wouldn't. He *is* possessive, isn't he? (*Looks at her admiringly*) And now that I meet you I can see why!

FAITH   (*Off balance, embarrassed*) Thank you. This is my brother Willard.

WILLARD   We've met.

GILIAN   (*Takes him in*) Yes. But you were a boy then— you were . . .

WILLARD   I was eighteen, to be exact.

30

GILIAN   I remember. Of course I remember. That meeting was unfortunate. So sad. But future ones needn't be. Need they? (WILLARD *laughs*. GILIAN *turns to* FAITH *in wonder*) But he's the image of Craig, isn't he? Just look at photographs of your father young. It's startling the resemblance. Everything of his father. (*Stares at* WILLARD) Yes. Everything!

WILLARD   Everything except the effrontery of his genius.

GILIAN   I know you both dislike me. I know you both think of me as a kind of monster. But I'm not really. Get to know me. (*She laughs—a silvery, tinkling laugh —to both of them*) I'll meet you more than halfway, I promise you.

FAITH (*Wanting to get out of the room*)   Willard—please —I'm late . . .

WILLARD   O.K.
          (FAITH, *very disturbed, goes out.* WILLARD *lingers a moment*)

WILLARD (*To* GILIAN)   It's really unjust, you know, that you should be beautiful.

GILIAN (*Her eyes on him*)   But, dear Willard, injustice is the essence of everything, isn't it? Isn't it immature—to expect justice? But then, in many ways, your father was immature, wasn't he? So you're your father's son in that way too.

WILLARD (*His eyes on her, spelled by her*)   I can see why he loved you. I can see why he was obsessed by you.

GILIAN   But he wasn't, was he? He left me.

31

WILLARD   I can see why he did that too.
> (WILLARD *goes out. She stands looking after him. She smiles to herself; she is pleased at the effect she has had on him. A moment later,* WILLARD *comes back. They stand looking at each other, spelled by each other*)

GILIAN (*Smiles at him*)   Nice to see you again!
> (FAITH *appears in the doorway for a moment. She is very tense, disturbed*)

FAITH   Willard—I'll be late . . .

WILLARD (*Without taking his eyes from* GILIAN'S)   Go on without me. I'll stop by at the theatre.
> (FAITH, *burned up, goes without a word, shutting the door after her*)

GILIAN   The last time too—I wanted to see you again. The last time too, I was sorry when they took you away. I showed you that, didn't I? You knew that, didn't you? (*He keeps staring at her, saying nothing*) I remember now—so vividly—what happened, exactly what happened —so vividly. Do you?

WILLARD   I remember it differently—at different times.

GILIAN   You came that day—with a sinister motive, didn't you? (WILLARD *keeps staring at her*) Quite frightening it was. You frightened me when you burst in. You looked quite wild. Obsessed.

WILLARD   Did I?

GILIAN   You came to kill your father. I saw it in your eyes when you came in. But for me you might have done it.

It wouldn't have been nice—would it? It wouldn't have been—useful, would it? You hated me too. I saw that too—in your eyes. Though it was your father you struck down, it was me you wanted to strike down.

WILLARD Do you think so?

GILIAN Yes. You hated me. You wanted to kill me too. Was it because I made your father happy?

WILLARD I don't remember it that way.

GILIAN You blamed me, didn't you, for your brother's suicide? I understand it. But it wasn't just—not really just.

WILLARD (*A simple query*) No?

GILIAN You're older now. You're a grown man now. Perhaps you can be more objective.

WILLARD If you want me to be objective, I'll try to be objective.

GILIAN Weren't you jealous and resentful—all you children—that at last, after his terrible life, your father had found happiness with me? Weren't you?

WILLARD (*Stubbornly*) That's not how I remember it.

GILIAN Your brother kept pestering me on the telephone —to put your father on so he could unload his petty little troubles on him. Your father was in a fragile state —begging to be left alone—trying to work. He didn't want to be disturbed . . . (*With a half-smile*) except by me. I tried to do what he wanted. To give him the isolation he craved. Was it wrong of me to do that? (WILLARD

33

doesn't answer—he keeps staring at her) I wish you'd say something!

WILLARD Nothing occurs to me.

GILIAN (*After a moment*) I have to tell you, Willard, if I had it to do over again, I'd do exactly the same.

WILLARD Would you?

GILIAN I had kept from your father the news of your brother's suicide. There was a blizzard and I told him the papers hadn't come. So he never knew. I was guarding his peace of mind. He never knew—till you broke in and told him. You said to him something you shouldn't have said. He never got over it—what you said.

WILLARD What did I say?

GILIAN (*Apologizing for him*) Of course you were young. You were very, very young. You accused your father: "In your works you are a great humanitarian," you said, "but your avocation is infanticide."

WILLARD That does sound young.

GILIAN And then you struck him. He fell to the ground. For a moment I thought you had killed him. You must have thought so too. Because you began to cry. That touched me—when you cried. I felt a rush of pity for you.

WILLARD (*Dryly*) Still—you sent for the police.

GILIAN I had to. We were so isolated there. I thought Craig might die. What could I do when you broke in? I'd been reading to him quietly. He always asked me to

34

read aloud to him what he'd written. He wanted me—
and only me. Well, I gave him what he wanted. I tried.
I protected him from inroads from the outside. I'll admit
I found you—all of his children by my predecessors—
rather a bore. I felt that you were parasites on his fame.
You all meant nothing to him and I was everything to
him. Can't you see it from my point of view?

WILLARD (*Carefully, controlling himself*)   I will make an
effort—to stretch objectivity to the breaking point.

GILIAN   My life wasn't easy, you know.

WILLARD   Well, you had a pretty good run, didn't you?
Living in rented palaces all over the world, holding
hands with fame . . .

GILIAN   Craig was wonderful, but he was tiresome too.
I love life and people and—and—

WILLARD   Life and people.

GILIAN (*Laughs*)   Yes. And life and people were the last
things your father wanted. He wanted to be shut away
from everybody so that he could contemplate his doom.
He insisted endlessly on being doomed. No compliment
to me, was it? I hated that side of him. And yet—the
other side—the creative side—that was wonderful. You
know I have always been attracted by productive men.
Their age meant nothing to me. Your father was thirty
years older than I was—but productive. All my husbands
—and all my lovers—have been creative men—artists or
writers . . .

WILLARD (*Who is documented*)   Conductors . . .

GILIAN Oh, that was very brief. He was a pompous ass— but he *was* a great conductor. God, he was boring when he wasn't conducting! (*A silence*) Do you think you'll ever forgive me? Do you think you will ever learn to forgive me?

WILLARD Is that important?

GILIAN Not really. Forgiveness—what a condescending word! Especially since—as I say—I'd do it again. You gave me an awful lot of trouble, you know. I can't tell you what it took—in the weeks that followed—to get Craig back. He was shattered. Still, I forgave you even then. Right then. Do you remember? Just before they took you away, I kissed you. Do you remember?

WILLARD In jail—I wondered why you did it.

GILIAN (*Smiles at him as if she might do it again. Lightly*) Because I felt like it. (GILIAN *goes to the flowers she has sent* CHARLIE. *Picks off a blossom. Goes to* WILLARD *and puts it into his buttonhole*) There. You look quite smart. Odd, isn't it? That we should come together again this way? That's what I find so exciting about life—that it is unpredictable. That is what I enjoy about myself— that *I* am unpredictable. Shall I ask Charlie to invite you to dinner?

WILLARD Thank you, no.

GILIAN Why not?

WILLARD I'm afraid that if he gives me dinner he will feel that he's done quite enough for me, and I am after him for more.

GILIAN Oh?

WILLARD A grant.

GILIAN I'll work on Charlie for that. I have influence with Charlie.

WILLARD (*With bite*) I'm sure you have!
(*They exchange a long look. She is smiling. His expression is inscrutable*)

GILIAN You still hate me, don't you?

WILLARD You must give me time. I'll study to be (*Manifestly putting quotes around the word*) "objective."
(*He goes out abruptly. She stands looking after him, still smiling. She feels the exaltation of having made a difficult conquest. She moves to the bar and starts to make herself a drink. Carrying the drink, she crosses the room to her comfortable, habitual armchair. On the cross she stops at the table, picks up her husband's novel, sets her drink down, opens it, looks at the inscription and reads it aloud*)

GILIAN "For Charlie, but for whom this book would have been finished much sooner!" (*She laughs her little, tinkling laugh*) Good old Charlie! (*She picks up her drink and goes to the armchair. Sipping her drink, a smile plays about her lips.* CHARLIE *comes back*)

CHARLIE Hello, pet. Been waiting long? Up talking to Seymour. Raving about you. I didn't know you'd met him at the Boardmans'.

GILIAN Thought I'd told you.

37

CHARLIE You didn't tell me. He's in an absolute dither about you.

GILIAN Why don't you ask him down to have dinner with us?

CHARLIE I did. He couldn't. Has to read. He's very conscientious, you know, about his homework!
(*He says this with an overtone of derision*)

GILIAN If he prefers reading to me he can't be in much of a dither!

CHARLIE He's shy. I think you overwhelmed him a bit.

GILIAN I found him most appealing. Gives the impression of being—vulnerable.

CHARLIE You like that, don't you?

GILIAN Don't you?

CHARLIE (*Smiles at her*) Yes. I do. Especially when, as well as being vulnerable, they are very, very rich.

GILIAN I got a bit the feeling—charming though he was . . .

CHARLIE Yes?

GILIAN That if he had the courage—*and* the virility—that he'd be a pansy.

CHARLIE Not at all. I've known him a long time and I don't think so at all. Nothing at all wrong with Seymour except he feels guilty and inadequate and he won't go to see Alvin.

GILIAN What if Alvin cures him of his inadequacy? Would that be good for you?

CHARLIE I have instructed Alvin to make him independent of everybody but me! (*She laughs. So does he*) But maybe you're right. Who knows? Never thought of that! Maybe that's why he's afraid to see Alvin.

GILIAN But how unenterprising! How childish! Why shouldn't he have the courage—especially with all that money—to be himself—or *her*self?

CHARLIE Well, I'm doing my best. He makes appointments with Alvin. He doesn't show up.

GILIAN He dated *me*.

CHARLIE Did he? Did he! Well, maybe if he sees *you*, he won't have to see Doctor Greer.

GILIAN (*Laughs*) Oh, Charlie, you amuse me more than anybody. When I know I'm going to have dinner with you the whole day takes on a bright, new face.

CHARLIE (*Testing her out*) Very good marriage that would be—you and Seymour. Come to think of it—perfect!

GILIAN (*Teasing*) Think I might convert him, do you? If he needs conversion.

CHARLIE I don't know. It wouldn't matter . . . (*By this time* CHARLIE *has poured himself a drink and sits cozily beside her*) When you come to think of it, Gilian! What are the most successful marriages you know? Especially in the arts—everywhere else for all I know. Between homosexuals. Absolutely happy.

39

GILIAN   But I don't qualify. It would be lopsided.

CHARLIE   I know lopsided ones too. Perfectly happy. Where the sexual interest is elsewhere, it lessens the area of conflict. If the ultimate objective of marriage— after sex goes—is companionship—well, they have it from the beginning, don't they?

GILIAN   But Seymour's married, isn't he?

CHARLIE   Just getting his divorce.

GILIAN   Do you know his wife?

CHARLIE   Oh, yes—charming—she left him for a skiing instructor. She likes to ski.

GILIAN   He hero-worships you. Never saw anything like it.

CHARLIE   (*Genially*) Valuable attribute, hero-worship. Gives the young something to which to aspire.

GILIAN   He says you practically saved his life. Was he drowning?

CHARLIE   In his mind he was. He did have a period at Yale—when he was suicidal.

GILIAN   And you?

CHARLIE   I stuck by him.

GILIAN   How?

CHARLIE   I tried to get him into my fraternity. They wouldn't have him because he was Jewish. I made an issue of it. I resigned from the fraternity.

GILIAN   That was noble of you!

40

CHARLIE (*In apology*) I was young!

GILIAN And tell me, darling, when you did this quixotic thing . . . ?

CHARLIE Yes?

GILIAN Did you perhaps have an intuition that someday —Seymour might come in handy for you?

CHARLIE (*Beams at her*) It was more than an intuition, darling. It was a plan.

GILIAN (*Delighted*) You *are* an artist, Charlie. An artist with people.

CHARLIE He was scared, Seymour—pathetic. He had this overwhelming, monstrous Napoleonic father of whom he was ashamed. Film tycoon. He was an America Firster, Seymour's father—the poor boy had a hell of a time even applying for Yale because Daddy said Yale was Communistic. His mother gave him the money to go . . . Daddy wouldn't. I knew his mother—a sweet woman. After Daddy grew great he naturally kicked her out.

GILIAN (*Sticks to the point*) But the idea for the Foundation—when did you get that?

CHARLIE The day I got kicked out and I had to think of *something*. Great institution Yale—you meet interesting people . . .

GILIAN Why were you kicked out?

CHARLIE (*Smiles at her*) None of your business!

GILIAN You are truly wonderful!

CHARLIE (*Smiles at her*) That is an understatement.

GILIAN But how could you have provided—so clairvoy-antly—for this marvelous, opulent, cushy job . . . how could you have known . . . ?

CHARLIE But they hang on every bush—these unhappy American gilded youths—they buy radical newspapers that bait the rich, they support fellow-traveling organizations that, if they obtained their objectives, would impoverish them, they're all masochists striving pathetically to expiate something or other. Seymour really had something to expiate! It occurred to me that he might atone for his father's assaults upon art on the silver screen by starting a foundation that would help impecunious artists. He did and it's a going concern, and Seymour tells me that he's never been so happy in his life. *He's* not the philanthropist. *I'm* the philanthropist —because I've made *him* happy!

GILIAN (*Casually*) How rich a millionaire *is* Seymour anyway? Multi, of course, but how multi?

CHARLIE Modestly multi!

GILIAN Then isn't this Foundation a terrible extravagance? Could he get out of it—if he got bored with it?

CHARLIE Now you are encroaching on classified material. Top secret.

GILIAN (*Smiles at him*) I see I won't get it out of you. I'll get it out of Seymour.

CHARLIE (*Amiably*) I'll advise him not to tell you.

42

GILIAN What do you bet I find out?

CHARLIE (*With an irony edged with apprehension, but very friendly*) In a contest of such a delicate nature, dearest Gilian, I would never bet against *you*.
(GILIAN *laughs. A moment's pause. She feels she perhaps has gone a bit too far—decides to change the subject. Points to the flowers*)

GILIAN You haven't thanked me for the flowers.
(CHARLIE *gets up. Goes to the flowers*)

CHARLIE Thank you, darling. Very sweet of you. (*As he reads the card*) Very neat, though as usual—inconclusive. (*She smiles. He comes back to her*)

GILIAN I met them. I ran smack into them.

CHARLIE Who?

GILIAN My stepchildren.

CHARLIE (*This does startle him*) You didn't.

GILIAN I did indeed!

CHARLIE I warned them. I warned them you were coming.

GILIAN Am I an epidemic?

CHARLIE (*Chuckling*) You certainly are! Well, how did it go? Was it awkward?

GILIAN (*Almost to herself*) I didn't allow it to be. I was quite startled by Willard. So like his father.

CHARLIE Well, there's nothing surprising in that.

43

GILIAN (*Silken*) And I congratulate you on Faith. I don't blame you, darling. I don't blame you a bit.

CHARLIE You offer me no alternative, do you? You can't be a bitch in the manger, can you, darling?

GILIAN Have you thought of marrying Faith?

CHARLIE Faith wouldn't like me at all if she knew me.

GILIAN I gather she does—*know you.*

CHARLIE I didn't mean it in the Biblical sense. It would bore me to be the sort of person Faith thinks I am.

GILIAN I'd hate it if you married her, but I wouldn't blame you.
(*A moment. He looks at her, decides to put out a feeler*)

CHARLIE She blames *you*! You are the obstacle, she says.

GILIAN (*Pleased*) Does she? Does she really?

CHARLIE (*Lightly*) And maybe you are.

GILIAN Oh, come now, Charlie! What would marriage give us that we haven't got now?

CHARLIE Concentration.

GILIAN Now, Charlie! You know perfectly well—we are both too talented to waste our skills on each other. We should distribute them.
(*A moment. He studies her*)

CHARLIE I have never had the margin to think of the present. I have always had to think of the future. I have to think of it now.

44

GILIAN Isn't Seymour—safe?

CHARLIE No one is safe. I have found—in my experience
I have found—

GILIAN (*Listening closely, in spite of his casual tone*)
Yes?

CHARLIE That you can't count on anyone—that everyone
is . . . unpredictable.

GILIAN Including me?

CHARLIE Especially you.

GILIAN Oh, come now, Charlie, you're my steady—as no
one has ever been. Who're you worried about now?

CHARLIE (*Looking at her—searching her eyes*) No one.
No one in particular.

GILIAN (*Absolved*) Well then!

CHARLIE That increases the potential of danger. It makes
me feel very—insecure.

GILIAN (*Laughs*) That's right. I'd hate you to feel secure
—and then have to disappoint you.

CHARLIE (*Stares at her, suddenly gloomy*) You'll disappoint me, all right.

GILIAN (*Reflectively*) I can't get over it—Craig—all those
common wives before me—and yet—those attractive children . . .

CHARLIE Are you an aristocrat, darling?

45

GILIAN   I've told you often enough—distinguished Southern family.

CHARLIE   Too bad they moved to Chicago!

GILIAN   Yes, that was unfortunate, but I was conceived, don't forget (*She kicks his foot*), in Charleston, South Carolina.

CHARLIE (*Lifts his drink to her*)   I salute the Southern aristocracy.

GILIAN (*Smiles at him*)   But I'm not in the least a snob. I know *you're* common, and yet I adore you. I have never believed, for instance, that your name is Taney.

CHARLIE   It isn't.

GILIAN (*Deeply curious*)   What is it? Tell me. Tell me, darling. I promise—I won't tell a soul. What's your real name?

CHARLIE (*With mock dignity*)   You don't know me well enough to ask me personal questions like that.

GILIAN (*She laughs. After a moment*)   Willard's after you for a grant, I gather.

CHARLIE   Faith's dunning me about it.

GILIAN   Are you going to give it to him?

CHARLIE   He's a lush.

GILIAN   So was Craig.

CHARLIE   Yes—but with a difference.

GILIAN   Give it to him. Seymour can afford it.

46

CHARLIE My job is to keep Seymour from making mistakes. (*Gives her a sharp look*) Willard and Faith both loathe you. Isn't it noble of you to intercede in their behalf?

GILIAN But isn't nobility a quality we both share? Think of your nobility in resigning from the frat. Craig despised you. You must know that, don't you?

CHARLIE Of course I knew it.

GILIAN And yet it didn't keep you from being warm friends, did it? Craig once said to me: "I like having Charlie around. I study him. He justifies me in despising the human race!"

CHARLIE He said it to *me* once when he was drunk. He was always on the qui vive for self-justification. I felt exactly the same way about him. And yet—in an odd way—I took comfort from his lapses. I thought: "You can be a man of genius and you can also be what Craig is!" (*With a disarming smile at her*) It consoled me for not being a man of genius!

GILIAN I do adore you, Charlie. You are perfectly honest —at least with me!

CHARLIE But Craig was useful to me—useful to the Foundation—his prestige helped get it started. But he disgusted me. He was all mixed up about sex, for one thing. He took it so *seriously*. He mixed it up with sin.

GILIAN I know—with all his wives and with all his girls, he was inexperienced in sex. His interest in it was morbid, guilt-ridden. He was a Puritan. Awful. There's

47

nothing more awful than a sex-ridden Puritan. Don't you agree?

CHARLIE I can have no opinion as I am only sex-ridden!

GILIAN (*Laughs*) You *do* amuse me, Charlie, more than anybody. You *are* funny!

CHARLIE Of course I'm funny. If I were sick I'd be a sick comedian.
(*They look at each other, smiling at each other in mutual appreciation and understanding. From upstairs we hear the austere, massive and passionate chords of Bach's* Fantasia *and* Fugue. GILIAN *listens*)

GILIAN Seymour?

CHARLIE Yes. He's always at the God-damn piano. Gets it out of his system that way. (*He makes a helpless gesture*) I love Seymour—but I have to admit—he's a bit of a jerk.

GILIAN (*Smiling a bit*) I don't agree, you know. I think you underestimate him.

CHARLIE (*Looks at her narrowly*) Do you think so?

GILIAN (*Listening to the music*) Yes, I think you do. I am sure you do. (*A moment. He keeps looking at her*) I am really very taken with Seymour, you know.

CHARLIE (*Lightly*) Are you?

GILIAN I think I am.

CHARLIE (*His voice sharp with irony—he feels a pang of jealousy*) He's lucky! (*A moment—he gives her a*

48

searching look) Maybe then I'll have to begin to worry about Seymour—

GILIAN   Maybe. Better than just being worried at large—isn't it?
   (*She slaps his cheek affectionately.* ANNA *comes in*)

ANNA   Dinner is served, Mr. Taney.

GILIAN   Good! I'm starved!
   (ANNA *goes out.* GILIAN *gets up*)

CHARLIE   I've got terrible news for you, Gilian.

GILIAN   (*Mischievous, knows what it is*)   Really? What about?

CHARLIE   Anna! She's leaving me. I suppose now you'll drop me. It will be interesting to see whether you drop me.

GILIAN   On the contrary—it only strengthens my hold on you.
   (*She entwines her arm with his and starts him toward dining room*)

CHARLIE   What do you mean?

GILIAN   Because Anna's coming to work for me! (*He stops, absolutely dazed*) So you see, darling, you'll be almost as dependent on me as Seymour is on you!

CHARLIE   (*Disentwines his arm from hers, stares at her*)   I'll—be—God damned!

GILIAN   (*Joyously*)   On the contrary, darling, you'll be well fed—in the style to which you've been accustomed!

49

CHARLIE (*He looks at her aghast*) This is really a bit thick! If you'd take Anna away from me, you'd take anyone away from me. Really, Gilian, you're capable of anything, aren't you?

GILIAN Of course I am, darling. So are you. That's what makes us such good companions, isn't it?
(*She links her arm in his again, and smiling at the really devastated* CHARLIE, *she walks him into the dining room, accompanied by Bach*)

Curtain

Act Two

ACT TWO

SCENE ONE

Scene: The same. Several weeks later. An afternoon in June.

At rise: SEYMOUR ROSENTHAL *is sitting at* CHARLIE's *big table. He is studying an application form.*

CHARLIE Highball, Seymour?

SEYMOUR (*Poring over the form, frowning*) No, thank you, Charlie.

CHARLIE (*Drink in hand, walks to table, sees his preoccupation*) You seem anxious. What's worrying you?

SEYMOUR (*Taps the form*) Brock Dunnaway. He wants a renewal.

CHARLIE I know. And as you see from my notation—I think we should turn him down.

SEYMOUR (*Troubled*) I know. (*He puts the form down, gets up, walks around, in quiet perplexity*) But I just hate to, Charlie. I just hate to.

CHARLIE Look, Seymour! We gave him a grant two years ago. He's turned in nothing. I don't think he ever will.

SEYMOUR He wrote the greatest novel of the First World War. He must be well over seventy. And he's working on a book which will summarize, he says, all his experience of life. It's considerable—that experience.

CHARLIE   I don't believe for a moment that he's working on it—or anything. He's just living off your grant.

SEYMOUR   He says—(*He returns to the application, picks it up*) he says that he's slower than he used to be—that he's become self-critical and even self-conscious—but he thinks that what he is doing now will surpass his early masterpiece. Makes sense, doesn't it? (*Anxiously*) Doesn't it make sense?

CHARLIE   He's faking. I don't think he's doing a thing. (*A pause.* SEYMOUR *resumes his pacing*)

SEYMOUR   But suppose he's telling the truth? Suppose he's agonizing—suffering over something—trying to get it out of himself—it can't be easy you know—at his age.

CHARLIE   He's very spry. Very lively. I get more laughs out of Brock than out of anybody almost. But you're not running your Foundation, dear boy, to support indigent writers. You're running it to get some gifted young people over the bumps. I say—turn him down. I'll do it. You don't have to even see him.

SEYMOUR   I asked him to come here.

CHARLIE   Good! I love Brock. He's so *nasty*! But turn him down.

SEYMOUR   He wrote one great book. Maybe . . .

CHARLIE   He *won't* do it again. He's a one-shot. Woods are full of 'em. They write one good thing and that's it.

54

SEYMOUR (*Pained*) I suppose you're right. I hardly know him, you know—have just spoken to him on the telephone . . .

CHARLIE (*Sees how painful this is for* SEYMOUR) If you want to help him out with a personal loan do it—but don't clutter up the Foundation. We can use that grant for better prospects, I assure you.

SEYMOUR O.K., Charlie. You're the boss.

CHARLIE (*Smiles at him*) Gracious of you to say so!

SEYMOUR I always take your advice. You know that.

CHARLIE (*Goes to the table, fishes for a form in the pile*) There's an application I've been asked to ask you to consider . . . might give him Brock's stipend, as a matter of fact . . .

SEYMOUR Who?

CHARLIE Willard Prosper.

SEYMOUR Any relation to Craig . . . ?

CHARLIE Son.

SEYMOUR Didn't he commit suicide?

CHARLIE That was his brother. This one . . . (*He taps the form*) hasn't yet. His chances, though, are rosy!

SEYMOUR Is he a writer?

CHARLIE He's a scholar. For all I know he can even write.

SEYMOUR What's his project?

CHARLIE Some son-of-a-bitch named Chamfort. (*Peers at the application*) Chamfort, Sébastien Roch Nicolas to be exact!

SEYMOUR (*Pleased*) Oh, that's very interesting!

CHARLIE For God's sake, Seymour, don't tell me you know who the hell he is!

SEYMOUR (*With diffidence*) I'm interested in that period —I've read quite a bit in it.

CHARLIE Is he worthy of our attention?

SEYMOUR He was a fascinating man. Very witty. Lived by his wit.

CHARLIE That wants doing! *I* live by my wits. It's easier when it's plural, if you know what I mean!

SEYMOUR (*Quotes*) "I am leaving this world where your heart will be broken unless it's made of bronze." He was as good as his word. He killed himself.

CHARLIE Well, Willard's heart isn't made of bronze either, so he'll probably imitate his hero. He won't be missed much—except by his sister.

SEYMOUR A son of Craig Prosper's—I'd like to meet him.

CHARLIE You won't be able to avoid it. His book's half done, his sister tells me.

SEYMOUR I'd love to read what he's written.

CHARLIE (*With irony*) I think that can be arranged! I have to warn you though, Seymour . . .

SEYMOUR What about?

CHARLIE Willard's a lush. He's nuts. He's desperate—and he's got a good deal to be desperate about!

SEYMOUR (*With reverence*) Craig Prosper's son!

CHARLIE Yah, and I don't think he'll ever get over it!
(MISS SAUNDERS *pops her head in*)

MISS SAUNDERS Mr. Dunnaway to see Mr. Rosenthal.

CHARLIE Send him in. Any luck with a cook, Miss Saunders?

MISS SAUNDERS Not so far. I've interviewed dozens.
(*She goes out.* CHARLIE *groans*)

CHARLIE God, how I miss Anna! Gilian took her away. She takes everything away. I promised to get Gilian out of a boring cocktail party. I'll be right back. Stick around. We'll have dinner together—(*Starts to go—stops*) Now, you're sure you can handle Brock? You're sure you can be firm?

SEYMOUR (*Smiles*) I think so.

CHARLIE (*Pleased with him*) It's a tough world you know, Seymour. Be back in a jiff.
(CHARLIE *goes.* SEYMOUR *sits at the table—he keeps staring at the Chamfort dossier*)

SEYMOUR (*To himself*) Prosper. Willard Prosper . . .
(BROCK DUNNAWAY *comes in. He is a spry seventy, little, nimble, with a sharp, glittering eye. He has a genial smile, a genial manner. He speaks with beautiful diction and great precision.* SEYMOUR *rises to greet him*)

57

SEYMOUR (*Shyly*) I'm Seymour Rosenthal.

BROCK It is very good of you to see me. You have been
my benefactor for two years and I am glad of the opportunity to thank you personally.

SEYMOUR It has been an opportunity for us, Mr. Dunnaway. Your novel was my bible when I was young.
Wouldn't you like a drink?

BROCK Thank you very much. I would.
  (SEYMOUR *goes to the bar to mix him a drink*)

SEYMOUR Scotch—martini . . .

BROCK Scotch on the rocks would be fine.

SEYMOUR That's easy . . . do sit down . . . (*Points*)
That's the comfortable chair—Charlie's . . .
  (*He smiles and so does* BROCK, *in a somewhat win-
try way. He ensconces himself in the chair*)

BROCK I knew your father quite well, you know.

SEYMOUR (*Wryly*) So did I!

BROCK He was most amusing.

SEYMOUR I didn't always find him so.

BROCK Put on a great show. Always acting. I enjoyed
him! (SEYMOUR *brings* BROCK *his drink*) Thank you
very much. I remembered—coming up here—I remembered . . .

SEYMOUR (*Politely*) Yes?

BROCK It was in your father's office that I read my
obituary.

58

SEYMOUR (*With a shy attempt at humor*) Was it favorable?

BROCK (*Smiles*) It was laconic. The first time I came to Hollywood—as a kind of official guest—to advise on the filming of my book—I got a great reception. Lunch in the executives' dining room—a bang-up dinner at your father's house . . . It was in the great days—when the industry was number five—right after General Motors.

SEYMOUR I was very young. But I remember when you came.

BROCK On my second visit, though, there were no bouquets. I telephoned your father and he invited me to his office. I came in the hope of a job, but your father said nothing about that. He just sat there behind that hemispheric desk, encircled by that rosary of telephones, and entertained me. I saw quickly that I was wasting my time—which wasn't worth much—and his—which was worth a good deal. Then he had an important telephone call—I suspected that it was contrived so he could get rid of me. He excused himself—said he'd be right back. While he was gone I entertained myself by going behind his desk and sitting in the papal chair. I picked up that little bust of Napoleon . . .

SEYMOUR (*With bitterness at last*) Father was very addicted to Napoleon. He was terribly disappointed in me —when he realized I was never going to be Napoleon.

BROCK On his desk also—was my obituary. (BROCK *pauses*) It was a mass obituary. It was a sheet of plain yellow paper headed in caps—WRITERS AVAILABLE.

59

Now as you know, in Hollywood, in those throbbing days, to be available was automatically to be undesirable. I looked down that list. It was a necrologue—playwrights who had had one success, novelists who had had one success—like myself. I couldn't remember who most of them were; I couldn't then remember who I was. Scott Fitzgerald was on that list. I took comfort in that. I knew then that Scott was doomed because he was available, but I felt he might survive elsewhere. I took comfort in that.

(SEYMOUR *gets up—this story disturbs him*)

SEYMOUR (*Half to himself*) Imagine a world where Scott Fitzgerald has to win the approval of my father!

BROCK (*Sips his drink—cheerfully*) That's the kind of world it is! And it's not so bad, is it? I wish your father were alive. I'd like to tell him you're supporting me! Would he like that? Too bad Scott isn't alive. You could support *him*, who deserves it far better than I. If he were alive he wouldn't be as popular as he is now—and he'd need your help.

(BROCK *doesn't realize—or perhaps he does—how very difficult he is making it for* SEYMOUR. SEYMOUR *gets up, goes to the bar and pours himself a drink. He feels he needs it*)

BROCK (*While* SEYMOUR *is at the bar*) I have asked for a renewal of my grant. I realize that, so far, there isn't much to show to justify your continuing generosity. The idea that I am working on is one that I have been carrying around for many years. I want to write it before I die. I'd like to tell you a little about it.

60

SEYMOUR   I'd love to hear about it.

BROCK   It concerns itself with the violence of American life—the violence that seethes underground everywhere. Have you noticed that the great staple of our literature concerns itself with inherited grievances—inherited revenges? Between individuals—between races. My thesis is that our artists—since they are the most sensitive of the species—inevitably reflect that violence. That is why one of the most distinguished of us was so enraptured by bullfights. Sadism and sex. And all that nonsense about the moment of truth! There *is* no moment of truth. There are intimations of truth, but these are achieved by saints and mystics—not by bullfighters in tight pants.

SEYMOUR   (*Deeply impressed*)   I have often thought— I hope it won't sound pompous—but I have often thought . . .

BROCK   (*Encourages him*)   Yes?

SEYMOUR   People talk about disarmament. What's the good—when the individual himself . . . in his heart . . . is not disarmed?

BROCK   (*Smiles his wintry smile, he feels he has* SEYMOUR *in his pocket*)   Exactly so. Our artists—like the public, in general—know no tranquility. They know everything about life—except how to live. Therefore, they often kill themselves—if not overtly—by other stealthy means. If they can't kill themselves, they kill those around them— their wives, their children, whoever. Actually what I am doing is writing a novel about Craig Prosper, whom

61

I knew very well. I was with him you know in Italy at the end . . . I remember an odd incident.

SEYMOUR Yes?

BROCK We were staying in a little hotel on the Italian Riviera . . . we were sitting in his bedroom. Bottles everywhere. He was drinking like mad.

SEYMOUR What happened?

BROCK The little Italian maid came in to do the room. She was very young—not very pretty—about seventeen, I should say—didn't speak a word of English. Craig had no Italian.

SEYMOUR Formidable obstacle!

BROCK Craig had a plastic pencil-sharpener. He showed the girl that. She cooed with delight over it. You might think it was the seventh wonder of the world.

SEYMOUR (*Stuttering*) It's almost . . . it's almost . . . one doesn't want to hear . . .

BROCK Oh, but he didn't touch the girl. He didn't go near her. I think she would have screamed and run out if he had. He looked awful—bloated and dying and awful.

SEYMOUR What then?

BROCK He began making love to her in English. She was busily making the bed and smiling cooperatively. Craig sat in the chair by the window and told her, in English, and very specifically, what he was going to do to her. A fantasy of sex in four-letter words. The girl kept

62

smiling as if Craig was describing the scenery. He kept on and on with it until the girl left the room. She bobbed her head, said, "Grazie, Signore, buon giorno, Signore," and left.

SEYMOUR   It's very sad.

BROCK   I do hope, though, you won't publish this novel in my lifetime. Because if you do Gilian will shoot me. *My* way of committing suicide, you see.

SEYMOUR   (*Struck*)   Gilian . . . ?

BROCK   Now, please don't misunderstand me. Gilian is a very close friend of mine. I love her dearly . . . I find you very sympathetic, Mr. Rosenthal. Not as amusing as your father—but more sympathetic.

SEYMOUR   (*Absently*)   Thank you.

BROCK   That bust of Napoleon. They all worship Napoleon, these tycoons. They forget that their success is often sheer accident. I tell you this, my boy, while Napoleon remains a glamour boy and St. Francis a schnookle there'll be no hope for the human race.

SEYMOUR   (*He has made up his mind*)   Mr. Dunnaway . . .

BROCK   (*Kindly*)   Brock is my name . . .

SEYMOUR   Thank you—Brock. We will be most happy to renew your grant. I am sure I can persuade the board.

BROCK   And I am so taken with you that I may even finish it! (*They both laugh*) Most fiction is utter drivel. Remote from reality. But I *know* what I'm writing about.

63

I don't want to boast about past achievements—very tiresome in an old man—but I had my days of violence. I am an extinct volcano now, but when I was active . . .

SEYMOUR (*Smiles*) Did you ever kill anyone?

BROCK (*Smiles back*) I tried! On one enchanted evening —I had had a bad day at my desk—I knocked my first wife out cold. It looked bad for her for a time—and for me too!—I was indicted for assault—but fortunately my wife had a wonderful doctor. Not only did he cure her, but he married her. They've lived happily forever after. And my son, thank God, is a nuclear physicist—that's the snug thing to be in our time, don't you think so?

SEYMOUR (*Disturbed*) Evidently . . .

BROCK My juiciest character will be Gilian!

SEYMOUR Really?

BROCK She is what the French call an *allumeuse*. Ignites without satisfying. She doesn't sleep with anybody, you know. Just likes to hear about it.

SEYMOUR I'm learning a lot about life!

BROCK There's a great deal to learn, my boy.

SEYMOUR But tell me—why do you want to do this? Why do you want to write this book?

BROCK (*With his genial smile*) My revenge—for being old!
　　　(MISS SAUNDERS *looks in*)

MISS SAUNDERS A Mr. Lorch to see Mr. Taney.

64

SEYMOUR   Has he an appointment?

MISS SAUNDERS   Yes. He has. I forgot to remind Mr. Taney.

SEYMOUR   Well, Mr. Taney will be back in a minute. Ask him to come in.
(MISS SAUNDERS *disappears*)

BROCK   Another applicant?

SEYMOUR   Haven't the faintest idea.
(HARRY LORCH *comes in. He wears dark glasses. He is a rugged man with touseled hair, sloppily dressed; he's just not interested in that sort of thing. He has the broad chest of a man who has spent his life playing wind instruments and the assurance of knowing that he is master of his art. Also he has the confidence of knowing that he can interpret beautifully what is, for him, the greatest art that exists in the world*)

SEYMOUR   I am Seymour Rosenthal. This is Mr. Dunnaway. Mr. Taney will be here any minute.

LORCH   I have an appointment for four-thirty. (*Looks at his wrist watch*) It's just four-thirty. When I make an appointment for four-thirty I'm always there—on the dot.

SEYMOUR   (*Apologetically*)   Well you know, Mr. Lorch, traffic . . .

LORCH   (*Combatively*)   I *allow* for traffic.

BROCK   Are you a beat novelist, Mr. Lorch?

LORCH   I'm a bassoonist.

BROCK Ah! I'm so pleased.

LORCH What are you pleased about?

BROCK That you are something sanitary.

LORCH What made you think I wasn't?

SEYMOUR (*Smiles at* LORCH) I do implore you, Mr. Lorch, do not question Mr. Dunnaway too closely!

LORCH But I want to know what made him think I was one of those—what he said . . .

BROCK (*Dreamily*) Somehow, for a fleeting moment—

LORCH (*Hot under the collar*) I don't know who you are and I don't care—but I can tell you this—you're way off base.

BROCK (*To* SEYMOUR, *sadly*) And I pride myself on my observation!

SEYMOUR (*Intervening to protect* LORCH) Please, Mr. Lorch, don't mind anything Mr. Dunnaway says. His bark is worse than his bite.

LORCH Couldn't matter less to me whether he barks *or* bites. (*Looks at his watch again*) It's four-forty. He's ten minutes late!

BROCK As a musician you are, of course, a slave to time. You live on time, don't you? May I ask, Mr. Lorch, what orchestra you play in?

LORCH I'm in the orchestra at—oh, that show at the Shubert.

SEYMOUR (*Surprised*) The Prosper play?

66

LORCH That's right. That's where the union put me.

BROCK Such a sad play, isn't it? That poor hero—his mother had such an effect on him that he's impotent. It seems to me that all the heroes—in all the plays I see—are impotent; and yet offstage the pundits are worried about the population explosion. Paradoxical—isn't it? How do you account for it, Mr. Lorch?

LORCH Don't ask me. I haven't seen the play and I don't want to see it.

BROCK (*Gets up*) But this is very illuminating, Seymour! We flatter ourselves that art and literature are vital forces. They are, I have long believed, of very little importance except to the practitioners. The great public is interested only in sex and violence, which they get on television and in movies.

LORCH (*To* BROCK) You're wrong, wise guy. The house is sold out every night with suckers who like gab. But I tell you this—ten bars of Bach are worth more than all the plays on Broadway.

BROCK Ah, you like Bach!

LORCH He's my passion. You sized me up. Now I'll size you up.

BROCK Please do.

LORCH I bet you a dollar to a dime you can't read a note of music.

SEYMOUR (*Pleased*) You've met your match, Brock.

67

LORCH (*Truculent, persists*) Ten to one you can't read a Bach score.

BROCK Well, if it were illustrated I might struggle through it. I'm afraid you're a narrow specialist, Mr. Lorch. Tell me, is your entire horizon bounded by Bach?

LORCH You've got me wrong again, smarty. I like Beethoven almost as much as Bach!

BROCK (*Enjoying himself—*LORCH *is a natural for him*) How do you feel about the pictorial arts?

LORCH I can live without 'em. (CHARLIE *comes back.* SEYMOUR *heaves a sigh of relief.* CHARLIE *doesn't at once notice* LORCH. LORCH *steps forward*) We had an appointment for four-thirty. It's twenty minutes to five.

CHARLIE (*Remembers*) Oh, of course, Mr. Lorch! I'm so sorry. I got tied up in traffic.

BROCK Mr. Lorch *allows* for traffic!

CHARLIE (*To* LORCH) I'm really terribly sorry. Faith has told me so much about you, Mr. Lorch. Mr. Lorch is a bassoonist.

BROCK We know!

CHARLIE (*To* SEYMOUR) Didn't you offer Mr. Lorch a drink?

LORCH I don't drink. I came to have a serious talk with you, Mr. Taney.

CHARLIE Certainly. I look forward to it! (*To* SEYMOUR *and* BROCK) That Gilian! What do you think? She *begged* me to get her away from that cocktail party. When I got there she was having such a good time I couldn't pry her away with a crowbar. She was with Willard moreover . . .

LORCH   Faith's brother?

CHARLIE   Yes. They were drinking together and very gay.

LORCH   I don't know who this Gilian is, but if she was making Willard drink she's not a good influence.

CHARLIE   That view of Gilian startles me! Brock, what do you think? Is Gilian a good influence or not a good influence?

BROCK   I don't know whether bad or good, but one thing I do know—she *is* an influence.

LORCH   (*Looks at his watch*)   I have an appointment at six and I like to be *on time*.

CHARLIE   Certainly. (*Almost pleading, to* BROCK *and* SEYMOUR) Gilian'll be along any minute. Do wait in the library. There's a fire in there. So much pleasanter than this stuffy office.

BROCK   As this charming Mr. Rosenthal has just renewed my grant, I have the leisure to accept your kind invitation.

CHARLIE   (*Looks at* SEYMOUR)   What? But we decided we wouldn't!

BROCK   Mr. Rosenthal is susceptible to charm!

SEYMOUR   Well, after all, you have the veto.

CHARLIE What good is a veto with a push-over like you! You're hopeless, Seymour!

BROCK (*To* LORCH) So pleased to know you, Mr. Lorch. I have been carefully avoiding Craig's play, but now I'll go just to hear you bassoon.

LORCH You won't hear it!

BROCK Why? Are you inaudible? You appear to have so much vitality.

LORCH We don't play—except pinochle. Union rules.

BROCK Now why can't writers have a union like that? (*As he goes out with* SEYMOUR, *carrying his highball glass in his hand*) There's no doubt about it, Seymour, if I had my life to live over again I'd study an instrument.
　　(BROCK *and* SEYMOUR *go out.* CHARLIE *faces* LORCH. *He had forgotten the appointment, and now all he wants is to get it over with*)

CHARLIE I'm sorry you won't have a drink, Mr. Lorch. Do you mind if I have one? I've had a hard day.

LORCH It's your bar!

CHARLIE (*He is already there and pouring*) Thank you! (*Armed with his drink he comes down and faces* LORCH) What can I do for you Mr. Lorch?

LORCH (*With sincerity—and a bit pitifully*) You can tell me the truth!

CHARLIE Suppose I don't know it!

LORCH (*Ominously*) You know it all right!

CHARLIE   If I know it—I'll tell it to you—within reason.

LORCH   (*He is suffering; it's very hard for him*)   About Faith.

CHARLIE   Yes?

LORCH   I've tried to fight it—I've done my best to fight it—but I love Faith.

CHARLIE   I don't blame you. She's lovely.

LORCH   Do you love her?

CHARLIE   I have great affection for her.

LORCH   I asked you—do you love her—are you in love with her?

CHARLIE   At times—yes.

LORCH   (*Begins to sweat*)   I asked you to tell me the truth.

CHARLIE   I'm trying.

LORCH   You're either in love with her—or you're not in love with her. Which is it?

CHARLIE   It's not as simple as that, Mr. Lorch. It really isn't. My life is very complicated. *I'm* very complicated.

LORCH   I asked Faith to marry me—

CHARLIE   What did she say?

LORCH   She said that while you're available and there's still a chance to get you—she won't marry anybody else. So why don't you?

71

CHARLIE Why don't I what?

LORCH Marry somebody else.

CHARLIE Can you suggest anyone?

LORCH (*Looks around*) Living in a place like this—and with your connections—it ought to be easy.

CHARLIE Forgive me, Mr. Lorch, but it is a most unusual request.

LORCH Tell me this . . .

CHARLIE Tell you what?

LORCH (*He is suffering*) I can't ask you. I haven't the nerve to ask you. I feel I haven't the right to ask you.

CHARLIE You want to know—is she sleeping with me?

LORCH Yes—that's what I want to know.

CHARLIE Why don't you ask Faith?

LORCH I'm scared to ask her. Willard says you are. That's what we had the fight about.

CHARLIE (*Pricks up his ears*) You had a fight with Willard?

LORCH Yes. About you.

CHARLIE Who won?

LORCH He gave me a black eye. That's why I'm wearing these glasses. He said I was stupid because I didn't believe what he told me—that you're sleeping with Faith. Of course, he'd been drinking.

72

CHARLIE (*Ironically*) Charming fellow—that Willard.

LORCH (*Takes him literally*) You can say that again! He's as good as they come. He's the best friend I've got.

CHARLIE Do all your friends give you black eyes? Is that why you like them?

LORCH (*Truculent*) Look, Mr. Taney, I'm Willard's best friend and he's my best friend.

CHARLIE But you seem to quarrel.

LORCH That was no quarrel. It was just an argument. Willard can't quarrel with me. I won't let him. If he quarreled with me he wouldn't have a friend in the world—because I'm his only friend. I can't leave him without a friend, can I?

CHARLIE (*Looks at him in astonishment*) Well, I must say!

LORCH So tell me right out—was Willard telling the truth or wasn't he? Tell me that and I'll go.

CHARLIE (*Sees a way to get rid of him*) Willard was telling you the truth.

LORCH (*Takes out a handkerchief, wipes his forehead*) That's all I wanted to know.
(*A silence*)

CHARLIE Did Faith know—that you're coming here?

LORCH No. I didn't dare tell her. I'm—I'm bashful with Faith.
(*He stops; he is devastated*)

73

CHARLIE (*Touched by him*) My dear Mr. Lorch—may I call you Harry? (*Smiles*) I keep hearing from Faith—about Harry. She's very devoted to you.

LORCH Some devotion!

CHARLIE But she is.

LORCH Are you going to marry Faith?

CHARLIE I think it most unlikely.

LORCH Why do you sleep with her then?

CHARLIE My dear Harry. That query—to say the least of it—is unchivalrous.

LORCH (*Starts to go*) Well, you've answered my question. Thanks, I suppose. Goodbye.

CHARLIE Let's talk about it a minute.

LORCH What is there to talk about? I'm never going to see her again.

CHARLIE How intolerant! Why?

LORCH Because I'm not like you. I'm not in any doubt about whether I love her or don't love her. I *know*!

CHARLIE But I've told you—it's not likely I'll marry Faith. Keep her friendship. She may then marry you.

LORCH I couldn't. I couldn't marry her now—even if she'd have me.

CHARLIE Why not?

LORCH It's the way I was brought up, I guess. I couldn't marry an immoral girl.

74

CHARLIE Immoral! What an old-fashioned word.

LORCH To me, Mr. Taney, it ain't old-fashioned. It means something.

CHARLIE Do you consider yourself a moral man, Harry?

LORCH By and large. Oh, I don't mean I've never had anything to do with a woman. I have. But we always knew what it was. I never promised any girl anything beyond just—I mean she knew what she was doing and I knew what I was doing.

CHARLIE There are all kinds of morality, aren't there? Forgive me, Harry, but I consider you a most immoral man.

LORCH What do you know about me? I've never done anything to anybody.

CHARLIE You are a featherbedder. You sit below the stage in a theatre, not playing, not performing any service, pure parasitism, and you have no embarrassment, evidently, at taking pay for doing nothing. I consider that immoral, profoundly immoral.

LORCH But that's the union. Got nothing to do with me.

CHARLIE It has everything to do with you. If you were a moral man you'd resign from the union.

LORCH (His dander up) Look, Mr. Taney, I spent years learning to play the bassoon. I worked my head off. I'm one of the best. If they wanted me to play, I'd play. I'm part of the total musical accomplishment of this country and I deserve to be subsidized. Don't forget— we bassoonists haven't got ASCAP.

75

CHARLIE I think Faith is a profoundly moral person—one of the few I know.

LORCH After what you just told me—how can you say that?

CHARLIE Even in the comparatively trivial realm of sex, Faith isn't immoral—she is simply—amoral.

LORCH (*Helpless*) What does that mean?

CHARLIE It simply means that Faith doesn't accept the code that says sexual indulgence is a sin. To be promiscuous just isn't sinful to her, that's all.

LORCH If every girl behaved like that what becomes of the family?

CHARLIE It will march on, I promise you. Don't give it another thought!

LORCH Willard told me you're a terrible man . . .

CHARLIE (*Interested*) Oh? What's Willard got against me?

LORCH I guess what you're doing to his sister.

CHARLIE Is he in a position, do you think, to be censorious?

LORCH He's a wonderful man. He's got a weakness—but he's a wonderful man.

CHARLIE (*With asperity*) Don't you think, before he criticizes other people, that he should conquer that weakness? Now mind you, Harry, I am not criticizing *him*.

76

I believe that everybody should be allowed to go to hell in whatever manner he finds most agreeable.

LORCH (*In wonder*)   I can't get over it . . .

CHARLIE   What?

LORCH   That a girl like Faith . . .

CHARLIE   Well?

LORCH   Should go for a feller like you—I can't get over it. (*A moment. He broods*) Well, I'm a dead duck. That's for sure.

CHARLIE (*Tries to buck him up*)   Not at all. Really, Harry! Be more flexible. Life is flexible. Things change. It can easily happen—I assure you—that Faith will switch from a feller like me to a feller like you. She likes you very much. That I know!

LORCH (*Inconsolable*)   It's the first time I ever wanted to marry anybody. First time I was sure. I had such dreams—married to Faith. Getting up chamber-music parties. Faith serving drinks and sandwiches to the musicians. All up in smoke! She likes music, you know, Faith. She understands music. She's just about—perfect. Except for you!

CHARLIE   Persevere. Tell her that you know and that you understand.

LORCH   But if she's promiscuous—and you said it yourself —how do I know some other feller won't come along?

CHARLIE   You say you love Faith. You are deceiving yourself. It appears that you love her—with reservations.

77

LORCH We don't speak the same language.

CHARLIE I'm afraid that's true. Too bad. (*He goes to the desk, picks up a dossier to convey that he is a busy man*) And now, my dear Harry, I'm afraid that I really have to get back to work.

LORCH (*Sunk in gloom, looks at his wrist watch*) And I've got an appointment at six.
(GILIAN *comes in*)

CHARLIE Oh, Gilian! This is Mr. Lorch. He's just leaving. Mrs. Prosper.

GILIAN (*Very warmly*) How do you do?

LORCH Mrs. Prosper. Are you Faith's aunt?

GILIAN Do I look like an aunt?

LORCH I know Faith's mother is dead.

GILIAN I'm her stepmother.

LORCH (*Charmed by her*) Why doesn't Faith ever bring you around?

GILIAN Around where?

LORCH To my place. For chamber music.

GILIAN I love music. I'd adore to come.

LORCH I'll tell Faith to bring you. (*Looks at his watch*) I've got an appointment at six.

CHARLIE I know! So have I!

LORCH (*As he goes—in tribute to* GILIAN) That's a great little girl, Mrs. Prosper. She don't go for me. She goes for our friend Mr. Taney here. But she's a great little girl! She's a credit to you.

GILIAN   It's a credit I can't honestly claim!

LORCH   Some people are unlucky with their stepchildren, but you're the exception.

GILIAN (*Accepts the compliment graciously*)   Thank you.

LORCH   Goodbye, Mr. Taney.

CHARLIE   Goodbye, Harry. So nice of you to come. (*He sees him, with great relief, out the door; wipes his forehead and faces* GILIAN) Whew!

GILIAN   I don't believe it. I just don't believe it. *Are* there such people?

CHARLIE   There are. And Harry's one of 'em. The salt of the earth, I believe they're called. And yet you know, Gilian . . .

GILIAN   Well?

CHARLIE (*Decides not to pursue it*)   Never mind. Where's Willard?

GILIAN   Left me in a huff.

CHARLIE (*Lightly*)   Lovers' quarrel?

GILIAN (*Equally lightly*)   In a way.

CHARLIE   Why are you seeing so much of Willard?

GILIAN   For reasons of my own.

79

CHARLIE You beat me!

GILIAN He hates me. He's full of hatreds—you among them.

CHARLIE Oh? So Harry was saying. What's he got against me?

GILIAN (Amused) He despises you. Like his father, he sees everything in symbols. Craig was just mad about symbols. Willard sees *you* as a symbol.

CHARLIE That's very dignified! Of what?

GILIAN Oh, he says you're an opportunist and an adventurer. He sees you as a symbol of everything that's corrupt and meretricious in our society.

CHARLIE That's very flattering! But does it occur to this profound thinker that if I'm a symbol of corrupt and meretricious society, then society itself must be corrupt and meretricious?

GILIAN Thank you! I'll use that on him. I'm constantly defending you against him. I'm running out of defenses.

CHARLIE (After a moment) That fellow Harry—he was kind of touching, you know . . .

GILIAN Was he?

CHARLIE He's madly in love with Faith. He's a hick, of course, but rather sweet. He said Faith told him she couldn't consider him or anybody while I was—"available"—his word. And the odd thing is . . .

GILIAN Yes, darling?

CHARLIE   I'm exactly in the same position—with you—as Harry is with Faith. While you are—"available"—I can't settle down with anybody.

GILIAN   Dear Charlie! Are you proposing to me?

CHARLIE (*Faces her, seriously*)   Yes. I am.

GILIAN   It's very flattering. I'm touched.

CHARLIE   Gilian, listen . . .

GILIAN (*Smiles at him tenderly*)   You've never, darling boy, had my attention more completely.

CHARLIE (*In self-torture*)   I'm sick of being a funny man. I'm sick of . . .

GILIAN   Don't tell me you're going to stop being amusing. It would be a national calamity. What's the matter with you, Charlie?

CHARLIE (*After a moment—close to her—with complete sincerity*)   I wish you would, Gilian. I really wish you would. We understand each other so well. I think we could have a successful marriage. I really think we could. Say yes—so I won't have to ask you again. I want no longer to be available. I want to belong to somebody. I want to belong to you. Brock says I'm trauma-proof. I'm not. Not quite. I've never told you—or anyone— what I'm going to tell you.

GILIAN   Do. I love to hear things.

CHARLIE   I adored my father. He was a big, flamboyant, generous man. He spoiled me. He was murdered. Shot in his hotel room.

GILIAN   By whom?

CHARLIE   They never found out. That's why I left Yale. My allowance stopped—the day Father stopped.

GILIAN   (*After a pause*)   Give me a martini, will you, Charlie?
   (CHARLIE *goes to the bar, mixes a drink*)

GILIAN   It's odd you ask me, Charlie—just at this moment.

CHARLIE   Why is it odd at this moment?

GILIAN   You know, I've told you often—that I was never going to marry again.

CHARLIE   I know. But I am such a throbbing opportunity!

GILIAN   (*Laughs*)   You are indeed!

CHARLIE   (*Comes to her with a drink*)   Grasp it! Seize it! Before it vanishes.
   (*He bends over and kisses her while he hands her the drink*)

GILIAN   (*Most receptive*)   Darling. There's only one Charles Taney. Now that you've told me the rest tell me where you got that name.

CHARLIE   Out of a history book. He was a Chief Justice of the Supreme Court. I thought it was—toney.

GILIAN   And so it is! Toney-Taney! (*They both laugh*) I do adore you, Charlie, but you couldn't have asked me at a worse moment.

CHARLIE   (*Puzzled*)   Why?

GILIAN (*Very deliberately*) Because, as it happens, I *am* thinking of getting married.

CHARLIE (*Stunned*) Really?

GILIAN Really.

CHARLIE To whom?

GILIAN Seymour Rosenthal. (*A silence. He stares at her in incredulous astonishment*) I think I'd be ever so much better for Seymour—than your Doctor Greer.

CHARLIE You're surely not serious!

GILIAN Why not? I've been seeing him. I like him very much. And you know, he is very unusual. In my experience certainly. He is a saint. A crippled saint. Having been married to a devil it might be amusing, mightn't it, to be married to a saint? (*A silence. He stares and stares at her*) I know. It's startling. But isn't it rather—cozy. (*A silence. He is devastated. She sees it*) You're really disappointed, aren't you? I'm touched, dear Charlie. I really am. I didn't know your feeling for me—was so profound.

(*The telephone rings.* CHARLIE *goes to answer it*)

CHARLIE (*On the telephone*) Oh, Faith. Oh, sure—I was just going to call you . . . let's meet at the restaurant . . . yes, I did . . . I took it up with Seymour about Willard —he turned it down . . . I'm terribly sorry—I did what I could but he's my boss, after all . . . I know . . . I know how you feel. Anyway, I'll see you at seven . . . I'll tell you just what he said.

(*He hangs up*)

83

GILIAN   Was she disappointed?

CHARLIE   Terribly. Her brother means more to her than anybody, I think.

GILIAN   Was she terribly disappointed?

CHARLIE   Devastated.

GILIAN   *Did* Seymour turn him down?

CHARLIE   I decide . . . and I'm not going to give a grant to a psychotic who goes around panning me. I have to live up to the—symbolic value he attaches to me.

GILIAN   That's a nice arrangement between you and Seymour. He can blame rejections on you and you can blame them on him. (*She gets up to go into the library*) Who's in there with Seymour?

CHARLIE (*Absently*)   Brock Dunnaway.

GILIAN (*Pleased*)   That aging wasp. I love him. The more he insults me the more I love him. I'll ask him to have dinner with us. (*As she starts out*) Why don't you ditch Faith and join us?

CHARLIE   Can't.

GILIAN   It would be such an agreeable foursome.

CHARLIE   Can't.

GILIAN (*Pauses on her way*)   You're not angry with me— are you, Charlie? I couldn't bear it if you were.

CHARLIE (*He is seething with anger*)   Why should I be angry? The more I think of it—you and Seymour—the more—beguiling—it seems.

84

GILIAN (*In triumph*)   I told you! It's only startling—when it first hits you.
(*She laughs. She is at the door*)

CHARLIE   Ask Seymour to come in to see me for a minute, will you?

GILIAN   I will. That'll leave me alone with Brock. I'll be a pincushion of poisoned darts . . . But I can trust you, can't I, Charlie? You won't tell Seymour my designs on him? (CHARLIE *shakes his head*) I know I can trust you. If not you—who?
(GILIAN *goes out.* CHARLIE *is darkened by thought. He goes to the bar, abstractedly mixes himself another drink.* SEYMOUR *comes in*)

SEYMOUR   Yes, Charlie?

CHARLIE   Wanted a minute with you . . .

SEYMOUR   Awfully sorry you can't have dinner with us, Charlie. Gilian says you're busy.

CHARLIE (*Walks away from the bar, abstracted*)   That's right.

SEYMOUR   Anything wrong?

CHARLIE   No. Why?

SEYMOUR (*Smiles at him*)   You don't seem your usual gay self!

CHARLIE   It's that I'm a bit troubled about this grant to Willard Prosper. The more I think of it—the more I think it would be a mistake.

SEYMOUR   I'm sorry you feel that way. I'm greatly taken with the idea.

85

CHARLIE You've renewed Brock's grant. That was a mistake. I don't want to compound it with another!

SEYMOUR Couldn't we read what Willard has written and then decide?

CHARLIE It's probably good—even if it is, I don't think we should give it. I've been inquiring around about Willard, and he's absolutely no good. No character.

SEYMOUR Did Gilian say anything?

CHARLIE (*Dryly*) Plenty.

SEYMOUR (*Impressed*) Well, she's very keen.

CHARLIE Keen! She's clairvoyant!

SEYMOUR Hate to turn down Craig Prosper's son. Still—if you definitely think not . . .

CHARLIE I definitely think not!

SEYMOUR Well, that settles it, doesn't it? After all—you're the boss.
(GILIAN *comes back*)

GILIAN Seymour, I'm starved—and Brock's out of insults . . .

SEYMOUR (*Smiling*) May I go, boss?

CHARLIE (*Smiles back*) You may go.
(SEYMOUR *turns to* GILIAN, *who is in wonderful humor. As they start out,* CHARLIE *is standing at his desk, brooding over what* GILIAN *has told him. The lights dim.*)

Scene Two

Scene: The same. Several days later. Late afternoon.
At rise: FAITH *is walking around the room. She is very*
nervous. She has an appointment with SEYMOUR. *He*
comes in, a bit flurried. He carries WILLARD's *unfinished*
manuscript.

SEYMOUR   Miss Prosper . . . I'm terribly sorry . . . I hope
I haven't kept you waiting.

FAITH   Only a few minutes . . . (*Smiles to cover her*
anxiety) It only seemed long . . . because I knew you
were reading my brother's book and I'm terribly—
nervous.

SEYMOUR   I adore it. It's exquisite.

FAITH (*Overcome*)   Really? Really!

SEYMOUR   I have always been interested in the period of
the French Revolution. (*Goes to the desk, puts the*
manuscript on it) I wanted to like it very much as your
brother is the son of one of my heroes. I wasn't disappointed . . . it's delightfully written. It's penetrating.
And, most satisfying of all—

FAITH (*Agog*)   Yes?

SEYMOUR   It takes a wit to write about Chamfort, and
your brother is witty on his own. Made me think of
Strachey. More feeling than Strachey. Your brother
must finish this because . . . (*He smiles at her*) Oh, I

87

know what happened to poor Chamfort. But your brother must finish it because I can't wait to read it.

FAITH You mean then . . .?

SEYMOUR Tell your brother that the Foundation will be honored to give him a grant. Honored. (FAITH *can't stand it. She turns away*) What's the matter? Are you all right?

FAITH (*Her back to him*) I'm trying not to cry!

SEYMOUR Do you feel like crying?

FAITH I'm afraid it's too late.
(*She sniffles into her handkerchief*)

SEYMOUR (*Smiles*) When I feel like crying I indulge myself. I cry. When I'm alone, of course . . .

FAITH But I'm not alone!

SEYMOUR (*Starts to go*) I'll go . . . have a good cry. Then come upstairs and I'll give you a cup of tea.

FAITH (*Turns*) I'm all right. It was happiness. I can't possibly tell you what this means to me, Mr. Rosenthal.

SEYMOUR (*Factually—to give her a chance to get control of herself*) I gave the copy to Brock to read. Not for corroboration. For fun. Brock adored it. He says your brother writes far better than your father did. Brock was captivated by the style. Stylistically your father wasn't much, was he? All dynamic energy and furious indignation. No repose in him, was there?

FAITH (*Assailed by doubt suddenly*) Are you sure? May I tell Willard?

SEYMOUR Of course. I'll tell him myself.

FAITH (*After a moment, a prayer uttered aloud to herself*)
Thank God I did it. Thank God!

SEYMOUR Did what?

FAITH Went over Charlie's head. Sent the manuscript to
you.

SEYMOUR (*Surprised*) Hasn't Charlie read it?

FAITH (*Bitterness showing*) He's far too busy to read! He
told me you'd turned it down.

SEYMOUR (*Startled*) Did he? How could I have turned
it down when I hadn't read it?

FAITH He said you had. Something—I don't know what
—made me not believe him. Thank God I didn't believe
him!

SEYMOUR Charlie couldn't have meant it. You must have
misunderstood him.

FAITH You're the boss, he said, and you'd turned thumbs
down on it.

SEYMOUR Well, Charlie *is* the boss. He runs the Foundation.

FAITH (*Troubled again*) Well if he's the boss and he
just doesn't want this . . .?

SEYMOUR I'll have to clear it with Charlie, of course, but
I'm sure it'll be all right.

FAITH I'm not at all sure.

89

SEYMOUR   He's the decentest, kindest fellow in the world. I have reason to know—from personal experience. Once he's read it—I'm sure he'll be unable to resist it—(*He smiles at her*) as I was!

FAITH   He's awfully angry at me, you know.

SEYMOUR   Why?

FAITH   For doing this. For sending the manuscript to you.

SEYMOUR   Oh well, we'll save his face. I'll make him read it. I'll pretend to wait for his verdict.

FAITH   And supposing he still doesn't . . .?

SEYMOUR   Dear Miss Prosper. I will write your brother a letter—this afternoon, confirming what I have just told you. I'm sure Charlie will see it my way.

FAITH   It's terribly complicated . . .

SEYMOUR   Is it?

FAITH   Well—you know—Charlie and I—

SEYMOUR   I know.

FAITH   We had our first bitter quarrel—over this. And you know, Mr. Rosenthal . . . it was strange . . .

SEYMOUR   Please call me by my first name . . .

FAITH   May I?

SEYMOUR   Please . . .

FAITH   It was our first bitter quarrel—and in the course of it . . .

SEYMOUR Yes?

FAITH I began—I began to see Charlie in a different light.

SEYMOUR Oh?

FAITH A lot came out. A great deal came out.

SEYMOUR (*Taps the manuscript on the table*) But he spoke to me about this. He asked me to consider it. I don't quite see . . .

FAITH Something must have happened since . . .

SEYMOUR Have you any idea what?

FAITH No. I'm quite at sea. One thing did occur to me . . . though it's so fantastic that . . .

SEYMOUR What?

FAITH It came out—in the course of our quarrel—

SEYMOUR (*Helps her over the halts*) Yes?

FAITH It came out at last. He said it at last—what I've long suspected but couldn't bring myself to acknowledge . . . (SEYMOUR *says nothing, listens*) that it's Gilian he loves. That it's Gilian he wants. I was glad—at last —to have it come out into the open. I have to face it. I will face it. In fact, I have faced it. It's over between me and Charlie. (*She faces him*) I tell you, Mr. Ro— Seymour, if I can save Willard—if he can give up that miserable job and devote himself to finishing this book —to the work that I know he can do—it's all I care about. I have lived all this time in the terror—(*He says nothing. He is affected. He listens*) that Willard would do—what his brother did . . . what Father did . . .

91

SEYMOUR (*Very quiet*) Can you get your brother on the telephone? I'll speak to him. I'll tell him to quit his job.

FAITH I can't get him at the store. But we're having dinner together.

SEYMOUR I am free this evening. If you would both care to join me . . . after dinner . . .

FAITH I have to go to the theatre . . . And I know that Willard . . .

SEYMOUR (*Feels he has been too intrusive*) It was only a suggestion. You can bring your brother any time.

FAITH I know that Willard's meeting Gilian. This worries me too.

SEYMOUR Why?

FAITH There is hatred there. And that's what I meant just now. About Charlie. It occurred to me that he resents Willard—because he's seeing so much of Gilian . . .

SEYMOUR (*Very keen*) Is that why it worries you?

FAITH It's deeper than that . . . Seymour . . .

SEYMOUR Yes?

FAITH I feel you are a friend.

SEYMOUR I should try to be.

FAITH Willard sometimes talks wildly. About the "act" he calls it. About involvement. Commitment. For him, Gilian is the embodiment of evil. Charlie too.

SEYMOUR (*Surprised*) Charlie too?

FAITH   Yes. Don't ask me to explain. I don't pretend to chart the workings of Willard's mind. Any more than I could Father's . . . There's only Willard left to me now —and my brother's children. I have to fight to save them. Do I sound . . .? I suppose I sound—quite irrational!

SEYMOUR *(Simply)*   I sympathize.

FAITH   I've suffered all my life—under this dark burden. It's a kind of curse—an inherited curse.

SEYMOUR   Inherited?

FAITH   Yes. Inherited. You say you adored my father. I understand that. It is because you didn't belong to him. I have often thought—oh, if only I didn't *know* my father—if he were a stranger—and I could worship him from afar! *(She is frightened suddenly that she is jeopardizing* WILLARD'S *case)* I shouldn't be telling you these things. It will prejudice you against Willard. I'm crazy to be doing it.

SEYMOUR *(With strength)*   But you are quite wrong!

FAITH *(More lightly)*   We are a kind of Jukes family, you see—highly literate—and even creative. But a Jukes family still! My father's works are famous all over the world; and yet his grandchildren—except for the pittance Willard and I can earn—would be in a foundling home.

SEYMOUR   Does Gilian get it all?

FAITH   She gets it all.
      (A pause. SEYMOUR *feels he has looked into an abyss—he broods aloud)*

93

SEYMOUR   Brock says that we all live to revenge ourselves on somebody for something. To get even. It's a chilling view of life, isn't it?

FAITH   I suppose it's true.

SEYMOUR   (*Still thinking aloud*)   It takes different forms with different people, doesn't it?

FAITH   (*She understands what he means. Warmly*)   Your way is a blessing!

SEYMOUR   (*With self-excoriation*)   I can afford my way! But supposing I couldn't afford it?

FAITH   You'd have done something else—equally kind, equally—beneficent.

SEYMOUR   I wonder . . .

FAITH   (*Close to him, she adores him*)   I'm sure.

SEYMOUR   (*Musing over what* FAITH *has revealed*)   The eternal vendetta. Brock says the only way to end it is to administer a general anesthetic to the entire human race. I'm not quite as defeatist as that. Are you?

FAITH   (*Smiles at him*)   Not since I know *you!*
(CHARLIE *comes in. His manner is, as usual, casual and flippant, but inside he is seething with anger. He feels savage, murderous. He goes at once to the bar and starts to make himself a drink*)

SEYMOUR   Hello, Charlie.

FAITH   Hello, Charlie.

CHARLIE   Greetings! Drink anybody?

94

FAITH   No, thank you, Charlie.

SEYMOUR   No, thank you, Charlie.

CHARLIE   (*His usual manner—ironic jocularity*)   I must
brace myself for the tremendous conflict of authority
which I feel impending! (*Comes forward with a drink
in his hand—to* SEYMOUR) Who could ever have imag-
ined that Faith—of all people, Faith—would come between you and me! And in the wrong way! If it were
sex that would be fine. We'd fight it out man to man.
But interfering with my *authority*. Really, Faith—really!
   (*It doesn't quite get over, but they do their best to
   accept him as funny*)

SEYMOUR   (*Most conciliating*)   There seems to have been
some sort of misunderstanding. (*He smiles at* CHARLIE)
Faith is confused as to who's boss.

CHARLIE   So am I!

SEYMOUR   Miss Prosper, I imagine, didn't want to take
advantage of your personal friendship. She therefore
sent her brother's manuscript to me—(*He smiles*) to get
the objective opinion of—an outsider.

CHARLIE   For God's sake, Seymour, after all these years,
do we have to be *diplomatic* with each other?

SEYMOUR   I've read it, Charlie. It's lovely. You read it.
You'll agree.

CHARLIE   I don't read fragments. If it's lovely why doesn't
Willard finish it?

FAITH   (*To* CHARLIE)   You know perfectly well Willard
has a job which exhausts him. He has still a lot of re-
search to do. You know all that perfectly well.

CHARLIE He has plenty of time for other diversions, hasn't he?

FAITH What do you mean by that?

CHARLIE Look, Faith. I didn't ask for this. You asked for it. I've discussed this with you frankly. I now have to be equally frank about Willard with Seymour. I don't like to do it, but it's not my doing—it's your doing. You have acted—as the big guys say at the UN—unilaterally —and you leave me no choice.

FAITH You have a prejudice against Willard. What is it based on?

CHARLIE (*To* SEYMOUR) For one thing, he's an alcoholic.

SEYMOUR (*Mildly*) But, Charlie! If we condemned works of art because of lapses like that on the part of their authors we'd be greatly impoverished, wouldn't we?

CHARLIE (*Loses his temper a bit*) If his book is so good, why doesn't he quit drinking for a while and quit socializing and settle down to work and offer his book to a regular publisher? Why does he pester *us*? (*He takes a deep swallow of his drink*) I didn't ask for this, Faith. *You* did.

FAITH What did you mean by "socializing"?

CHARLIE You know what I meant. He has plenty of time to go around wooing his step-mother is what I meant.

FAITH (*Sharply*) I thought possibly that that is what you meant!

CHARLIE He goes around town panning me—panning this Foundation, which I represent. If he is so contemptuous of what we're doing, why does he apply to us for help?

FAITH   He's not applying. I'm applying. His book is applying.

CHARLIE   Seymour has so far kept up the polite fiction that I am running the Foundation. I'm the boss, he says. As the boss, I am turning this down. I am sorry to say it, Faith, but I find your brother personally repellent. I don't believe he has either the character or the stamina to finish this book. That is my last word on the subject. Except to say that I don't think it gentlemanly of you to have put me in a position where I had to say these things in front of Seymour!

(*There is a silence.* FAITH *turns to* SEYMOUR)

FAITH   Charlie has made his position clear. What is your position?

(SEYMOUR *is shocked by what* CHARLIE *has said; he is an agony of disillusionment which he can't bear to accept. His faint stutter becomes more pronounced*)

SEYMOUR (*Quietly*)   Your brother is going to get the grant.

CHARLIE (*Decides to frighten* SEYMOUR)   In that case you'll have to get yourself another director.

SEYMOUR (*Without lifting his voice*)   In that case I'll get one.

(*This shocks* CHARLIE—*it is the first time in their history that* SEYMOUR *has contradicted him on anything*)

CHARLIE   I don't think you mean that, Seymour.

SEYMOUR   You said quite a few things, dear Charlie, which are untenable.

CHARLIE For instance?

SEYMOUR For instance—that Willard is personally repellent to you. What has that got to do with it?

CHARLIE (*His voice rises*) I tell you he goes around town panning us. Panning the Foundation.

SEYMOUR That's his privilege. It has nothing whatever to do with the issue.

CHARLIE The funds at our disposal are not limitless. If we waste them on projects that will never be finished what will be left for decent, hard-working writers working on non-commercial books which they *will* finish? You are penalizing the decent ones to coddle the obscene ones.

SEYMOUR (*Increasingly pained*) There's nothing obscene in this book, Charlie. You are talking about a book you haven't even read.

CHARLIE I am talking about an author whom I know and you don't.

SEYMOUR (*Stumbles it out*) Please, Charlie, read the book. Then let's discuss it. You are under some sort of strain evidently. Your attitude in this—is not—characteristic.

CHARLIE Since college we've known each other—and this is the first time . . .

SEYMOUR I think that is a tribute to our friendship, don't you? That it *is* the first time . . .
   (*The telephone rings.* CHARLIE *takes the call*)

CHARLIE (*On the telephone*) Yes, Gilian . . . I'm in a meeting with Seymour . . . I guess I could. In fact—to tell you the truth—I welcome this interruption. I'll be right over. (*He hangs up. To* SEYMOUR) Gilian sends her love.

SEYMOUR Thank you.

CHARLIE (*Goes back to the table*) All right—I'll read the God-damn thing! (*He has resumed his customary bantering manner—to* FAITH) Did you think, Faith, that you could be powerful enough to make Seymour and me quarrel for the first time in our lives? (FAITH *does not respond*) Are you angry? I apologize for what I said about your brother. Would you deny me my little prejudices? They won't last long. You know that. I'm flexible and I'm tolerant. (*To* SEYMOUR) I'll call you tonight, Seymour—after I've read it.

SEYMOUR Good! You'll be enchanted, I think.

CHARLIE (*As he begins to go, he stops—he wants to hurt* FAITH) By the way, Seymour, did I tell you? Let me be the first to congratulate you.

SEYMOUR (*Quite in the dark*) On what?

CHARLIE Gilian is going to marry you. She expressed the intention. And when Gilian expresses an intention it presently becomes a reality.

SEYMOUR I'm very set up!

CHARLIE Who wouldn't be! *I'd* be! She always wanted my cook. She's got my cook.

99

(CHARLIE *goes. A silence between* FAITH *and* SEY-MOUR. *She goes to him*)

FAITH   I *can* count on your help in this, can't I?

SEYMOUR (*Automatically—he is in a terrible turmoil over the revelation he has had of his idol*)   You can!

FAITH   You see, I'm so worried about Willard—he's terribly nervous—disturbed. I live in the fear . . .

SEYMOUR   Yes?

FAITH   That he'll go over the line. Sometimes I . . .

SEYMOUR   Yes?

FAITH   He talks so wildly. I hope when you meet him that you won't misunderstand. He's harsh sometimes, and his harshness repels people, but I can tell you this—he is dear . . . he is honest . . . he is good. His need of love —his longing for love—is great.

SEYMOUR (*With a gesture toward the manuscript*)   I can tell from his book.

FAITH   I can't tell you what this means—not the money alone but the *reassurance*. It may save him. I bless you. (*A pause*) I've talked too much. I'm sorry. (*He keeps looking at her—says nothing*) I am sorry to have caused this rift—between you and Charlie.

SEYMOUR (*Desperately denying what he knows to be true*) Oh, no—it's not a rift—it can't be—we've been through too much together—Charlie and I for a—(*Grasps at a straw, brightens*) Didn't you notice—at the end—he veered a bit? Trust me—to win him over.

FAITH I do. I trust you. More than anyone else in the world—I trust *you!* (*Another pause. Finally*) Goodbye. (*She reaches out her hand. He takes it*)

SEYMOUR Goodbye.

FAITH Thank you. Thank you very much. (*Their hands are still clasped in their farewell handshake*) Before I go—I have to say—I feel I have to say . . . (*She stumbles for words*) That it is reassuring—to meet someone—who has some feeling—some sympathy—for people who . . . (*She wants to say "suffer"—she can't*)

SEYMOUR (*Quietly*) I have very little to offer—but, if I had—I would offer it to you.
(*She is startled, touched. Impulsively she lifts his hand, which she is still holding, to her lips and kisses it. She runs out of the room. He stands looking after her*)

Curtain

Act Three

ACT III

SCENE ONE

Scene: The same. Eleven o'clock at night, several weeks later.

At rise: CHARLIE, *in a dinner jacket, and with a flower in his buttonhole, is talking on the telephone to Doctor Greer.*

CHARLIE   Oh, Alvin . . . I'm glad I got you . . . since Seymour won't keep a date with you, why don't you come over here? . . . Believe it or not he's giving a chamber-music party . . . Since the mountain won't come to Mohamet . . . Well, if you love chamber music, so much the better . . . Oh sure, Gilian, Faith, her brother, everybody . . . Can't you chuck that? . . . Try, will you, Alvin? . . . Come as late as you like . . . but come!

(*As he hangs up,* GILIAN *and* HARRY *come in. Without the dark glasses we see that* HARRY *has fine eyes. His dinner jacket is a bit seedy, but he is now in his element, bringing chamber music to the Philistines. He displays the masterfulness of a crusader preaching God to the heathens.* GILIAN *is in a stunning Dior and looks radiant. She is in marvelous fettle*)

GILIAN   Hello, Charlie! Met Harry on the sidewalk. Wasn't I lucky?

HARRY (*Beams with pleasure*)   That luck is mutual.

GILIAN   Thank you, dear Harry.

CHARLIE (*On the way to the bar*) I know Harry doesn't drink. What'll you have, Gilian?

GILIAN Champagne, I think, Charlie.

HARRY (*Emboldened—to* GILIAN) It seems kind of funny to like your girl's mother the way I like you.

GILIAN (*Smiles at him*) I find you very sympathetic, Harry.

HARRY (*Warming up*) It's easy to be sympathetic with you.

GILIAN When I get back from Europe I hope to see a lot you.

CHARLIE (*With a sharp look at her—comes from the bar, gives her a glass of champagne*) Europe? When did you decide that, Gilian?

GILIAN Yesterday.

HARRY (*Released now to gaiety*) It's a shame you're going to Europe, just as we're getting chummy.

CHARLIE Good point, Harry! Work on her.

GILIAN (*To* HARRY) I'll call you when I get back. Then we can resume where we left off.

HARRY (*In full flirtation*) Well, with you going away, how will we get the time to get to the place where we can leave off *from*?

GILIAN But, Harry! You are very amusing!

CHARLIE (*To* HARRY) Are you going to play tonight?

HARRY   Sure. Second violin.

CHARLIE   Thought you were a bassoonist.

HARRY   Started as a violinist. But violinists are a dime a dozen, so I switched to the bassoon.

CHARLIE   Suppose the union hears about it?

HARRY   The union won't mind because we're playing for nothing.

CHARLIE   (*To* GILIAN)   Paradox, isn't it? When Harry *doesn't* play—at the theatre—he insists on being paid. When he *does* play, it's for free. How do you explain it?

HARRY   Because I love chamber music.

GILIAN   So do I. I can't tell you, Harry, how pleased I am to be here tonight.
    (SEYMOUR *comes in, elegant in his perfect dinner jacket. He looks at* GILIAN *approvingly*)

SEYMOUR   Hello, Gilian. (*As he takes in her dress*) Very decorative.

GILIAN   Thank you, darling.

HARRY   Oh, Mr. Rosenthal, could I just go up to your place for a minute and see that the music stands and the lights are okay? And I've got to sort out the music.

SEYMOUR   Certainly. Shall I go with you?

HARRY   Well, that would be a help just for a minute. As it's your apartment, you know the ropes.

SEYMOUR   (*Smiles*)   I hope so. By the way, Mr. Lorch, about the food: what do musicians like to eat?

HARRY   They like sandwiches. Big sandwiches. They like pickles.

SEYMOUR   Well, I think perhaps my cook can do better than that by them.

HARRY   They don't like fancy. They like sandwiches— corned beef, tongue and pastrami.

GILIAN   Can your cook be as primitive as that, Seymour?

SEYMOUR   She's adaptable. All right, Harry?

HARRY   Fine.
(SEYMOUR *and* HARRY *go out*)

CHARLIE   When are you going to Europe?

GILIAN   Sailing Wednesday.

CHARLIE   Paris?

GILIAN   Stockholm.

CHARLIE   Oh? Craig's play?

GILIAN   Yes.

CHARLIE   Mind if I come along—to Stockholm?

GILIAN   Oh, it would bore you. All that Swedish!

CHARLIE   That means you're taking someone else.

GILIAN   Yes.

CHARLIE   Who?

GILIAN   Seymour.

CHARLIE   Have you asked him yet?

GILIAN   Not yet. That's why I'd like you—when he comes back—to leave us alone for a bit.

CHARLIE   I don't want to discourage you, but I've found out something that may perhaps affect your program.

GILIAN   What's that?

CHARLIE   Seymour's taken by Faith. Isn't that odd? He's got a thing on Faith.

GILIAN   Darling! Have you lost *all* confidence in me?

CHARLIE   (*Studies her a moment*) No. No. I've never doubted that if you've set your mind on something— you'll get it. And after all . . .

GILIAN   Well?

CHARLIE   If you *are* determined to marry somebody, Seymour'd be better for me than anybody else. (GILIAN *tinkles a little laugh*) There've been irritations you know lately—between Seymour and me.

GILIAN   Oh? He's said nothing to me.

CHARLIE   As you know he's never questioned anything I've ever done.

GILIAN   Seymour's a natural hero-worshiper and you have always been his hero.

CHARLIE   There's been a rift in the lute. About a grant for Willard. I don't want to give it to him. Seymour does.

GILIAN   Assert your authority. Don't give in. To give in is fatal.

CHARLIE   He's stubborn about it.

GILIAN (*Sips her champagne*)   You be *more* stubborn.

CHARLIE   I am not, you know, in your Olympian position.

GILIAN (*Quietly*)   Go on the assumption that you are. Everything in life is courage. Everything in life is not to be afraid.
>   (SEYMOUR *comes back. He is feeling happy*)

SEYMOUR   One of those musicians really *knows* pictures! He appreciated my pictures.

CHARLIE (*To* GILIAN)   See how happy he is! The collector's beam!

SEYMOUR   Well, it *is* nice to have a guest who knows the artists without being told!

CHARLIE   Don't you think I ought to go up to see that they don't *steal* any? (GILIAN *and* SEYMOUR *laugh*) Oh, Seymour, I've invited Doctor Greer. He can make you comfortable on a couch and analyze you while Harry and his colleagues are playing Schubert!

SEYMOUR   Ideal conditions!
>   (CHARLIE *goes into his bedroom. There is a brief pause between* GILIAN *and* SEYMOUR)

GILIAN   I adore Harry, don't you?

SEYMOUR (*Warmly*)   I like him very much.

GILIAN   He has the perennial appeal of innocence.

SEYMOUR (*Somewhat ruefully*)   Don't I have that appeal?

GILIAN (*Definitely*) Your appeal is quite different! (SEY-
MOUR *is a bit embarrassed by this*—GILIAN *helps him out*)
Why don't you have some of Charlie's champagne? It's
very good champagne. And I wouldn't mind another
drop myself.

SEYMOUR (*Delighted to be employed*) Certainly . . .
(*He busies himself at the bar and presently refills
her glass. She smiles up at him*)

GILIAN You're very handsome.

SEYMOUR (*A bit embarrassed*) Thank you. I always con-
sidered myself well—rather—
(*He was about to say "unattractive"*)

GILIAN Yes?

SEYMOUR Shall I tell you . . . ?

GILIAN Please!

SEYMOUR You intimidate me. I don't feel entirely comfortable with you.

GILIAN I feel entirely comfortable with you.

SEYMOUR There are people I feel I understand. Faith, for
instance. But I have no notion of what you really are,
what you want, what you believe in.

GILIAN It is a great advantage sometimes, don't you think
so, Seymour, not to know exactly what one is doing?

SEYMOUR You make me feel hopelessly naïve. "Square,"
I believe they call it.

GILIAN   And yet you're scarcely likely to meet anyone who will be as frank with you—as I am prepared to be. (*A moment.* SEYMOUR *faces her*)

SEYMOUR   Why are you seeing Willard? What do you want from Willard?

GILIAN   Why don't you ask Willard what he wants from me?

SEYMOUR   He blames you for his brother's suicide.

GILIAN   I know, I know.

SEYMOUR   Willard is a very disturbed man. Faith is frightened. Aren't *you*?

GILIAN   I am afraid of nothing.

SEYMOUR   Doesn't that show—a lack of imagination?

GILIAN   But I'm not imaginative. I have no wish to be.

SEYMOUR   (*With passion*)   They have a grievance—Faith and Willard. They have a just grievance. Why don't you help them? Why don't you make friends of them? You could easily.

GILIAN   You say that because *you* are imaginative. (*With no trace of feeling—lightly*) I could never be friends with them. They hate me—as their father did. Also . . .

SEYMOUR   Well?

GILIAN   Willard loves me—as his father did. (*She leans forward a bit toward him*) These are facts, dear Seymour, and no amount of imagination will change them. And shall I tell you something else? I love Willard—as

I did his father. He is the image of his father. And when I get rid of him—I will have gotten rid of all of them. You say you don't know what I want. This is what I want.

SEYMOUR   How do you mean to do it—to get rid of him?

GILIAN (*Lightly*)   Since I have no imagination I allow for the improvisation of life.

SEYMOUR (*Half to himself*)   It is a morass . . . a swamp— a morass of evil.

GILIAN   But of course . . . What else?

SEYMOUR   Baffling . . .

GILIAN   Of course. What else?

SEYMOUR (*Again with passion*)   Surely life is more than improvisation—surely there is such a thing as will—and even good will—to steer the improvisation into some . . .
(*He stops; she helps him out*)

GILIAN   Vista of paradise?

SEYMOUR   Yes. The vista—even if not the paradise.

GILIAN   I do not long for paradise. Not even for a vista of it. I enjoy the *facts* of life. I am pleased with the facts of my own nature. I don't know all of them and I am in no hurry to find out. This adventure with Willard amuses me no end. The first time I met him he was eighteen and he came to kill me. He remained to make love to me. Well—isn't that—interesting? And it's still the same with him. He wants to possess me and he wants to kill me. Similar emotions, aren't they? (*He says*

113

nothing. He stares at her) I believe I shock you. I don't want to. I want to please you. I want to interest you. I am very devoted to you, Seymour. I like you no end. But, darling . . . I am going to tell you something I've never told anyone. There is a risk in it—a risk of alienating you. But then—I enjoy danger—or I wouldn't be seeing Willard.

SEYMOUR   Aren't there enough natural dangers in life—death itself—without going out of your way to court them?

GILIAN   But I don't go out of my way! Dangers—and other excitements—come to me. After all, it was right here in this room, on these scholarly premises, that I ran into Willard. Actually, I am very sedentary. (*She looks at him; he is deeply troubled*) I adore you, Seymour. You're a *good* man. (*With sudden revelation*) You know—it's just struck me—that's a *novelty!* (*They are both laughing. She holds out her empty glass*) Fill it. (*He takes the glass, goes to the bar, fills it, brings it back. A moment*) I'm a bit tight. Are you?

SEYMOUR   A bit.

GILIAN   Wonderful feeling, isn't it? Omnipotent.

SEYMOUR   Won't go as far as that. But I must admit—a little less inhibited than usual . . .

GILIAN   With you I'm not inhibited at all. Do you know how I was first—gainfully employed? (*He says nothing*) Posing in the nude for pornographic films. It was in one of those films shown at a stag-party in Chicago that my first husband saw me. He was an artist and he saw possibilities. I became his model and then his wife.

(*Pause.* SEYMOUR *is not shocked; he is saddened. It enlists him for* GILIAN, *as she knew it would*) Don't tell Charlie that. It wouldn't shock him. Nothing could shock Charlie. It would just annoy him that I told you something I wouldn't tell him!

(SEYMOUR *gets up. His face is grave. He looks down at her*)

SEYMOUR   Poor Gilian! Poor child!

GILIAN   It's odd my telling you that. I never thought I'd tell anybody that. I am constantly discovering things about myself. It's really rather fun. When I met Willard here the other day—when I found that he remembered that before I sent him to jail I kissed him—I felt a kind of thrill. Now isn't that odd? Vanity, I suppose. Sexual vanity. But you know what I discover lately—sex bores me. Too much fuss made about it altogether. What I want now, darling, is tranquility—and grace.

(*She looks at him. How tight is he? What is his mood exactly? How far can she go?*)

SEYMOUR   I've always been ashamed of being rich. The story you just told me makes me more ashamed.

GILIAN   I love being rich. Between us—we could be richer. You could indulge your good works to the limit. I don't in the least believe in them, but I'd be tolerant. It's a charming eccentricity—this benefaction of yours.

(SEYMOUR *is hardly listening to her—he is overcome by the vista of degradation her story has revealed*)

SEYMOUR (*Appalled—as if to himself*)   What kind of society is it—that forced you to that?

115

GILIAN   It's a good society. What's wrong with it? That film was a first cause which led eventually to Craig—and to my being asked, this very evening, to your house to listen to chamber music. It provides a wide margin for adventure—our society—and I like that! (*A pause, she sips her champagne*) I am feeling wonderfully cozy and happy and generally swell. How do you feel?
(*She smiles at him. Out of his preoccupation, he smiles back*)

SEYMOUR   At sixes and sevens.

GILIAN (*After a moment*)   Seymour . . .

SEYMOUR (*Absently*)   Yes?

GILIAN   You may be right, you know . . .

SEYMOUR   About what?

GILIAN   About Willard. I should, perhaps, stop seeing Willard.

SEYMOUR (*Goes to her again*)   I wish you would! I do wish you would!

GILIAN   I've reached that decision myself. I can't stop seeing him if I'm here. He pesters me—and I pester him. I've decided, therefore, to go away.

SEYMOUR   Oh?

GILIAN   Craig wrote a play—a play just for me he said at the time. I have the only manuscript. I sent it to a theatre man in Stockholm who is a great friend of mine. I am going over to see the world premiere. Why don't you come with me? Wouldn't it be fun?

SEYMOUR   That's very flattering . . . wouldn't I bore you?

GILIAN The moment you bored me I'd send you home.

SEYMOUR When do you plan to go?

GILIAN Right away. The *Drottingholm* on the fourteenth. That's next Wednesday. Such a nice boat. I took it with Craig when he went to get the Nobel Prize. I hate flying, don't you? No privacy.

SEYMOUR (*Sees the chance to do something constructive for* FAITH. *She is aware of it and uses it*) Very tempting. I've never been to Stockholm.

GILIAN (*Smiling at him*) Don't say anything to anybody. I'll book you a cabin.

SEYMOUR You're sure you want me?

GILIAN I am so sure that if you refuse I won't go myself. I'll keep up this dreary roundelay with Willard and God knows what will happen. Do come. Do get me out of this awful cat-and-mouse game with Willard.
(SEYMOUR *looks at her a moment*)

SEYMOUR (*Finally*) I'll come!

GILIAN I can't tell you—what a relief it will be for me!
(BROCK *comes in. He looks elegant and distinguished and spruced up in his dinner jacket*)

GILIAN (*Greets him*) My dearest enemy!
(BROCK *goes to her, bends over her hand, kisses it*)

BROCK My precious target.

SEYMOUR I am so glad you were able to come.

BROCK I never refuse invitations—from benefactors! It's so nice, for once, not to see Gilian at a funeral.

GILIAN It's true, you know, I'm always running into Brock at funerals.

SEYMOUR Whose?

GILIAN This morning—Clyde Enright's . . . and last week at . . . whose was it, Brock?

BROCK I forget. But you know—I was really very fond of Clyde Enright . . . I've known him for forty years. He was perhaps the gayest member of the international homosexual set, to which an Oxford wit has applied the generic appellation: the Homintern. I'm an outsider myself but I have always had an *entente cordiale* with some of its most distinguished members. They like me! I remembered this morning in church while the organ was playing. I was with Clyde in Florence. We went to the Uffizi. You know that great macabre sculpture stretched out on the floor called The Hermaphrodite? Clyde looked down at it, turned to me and said enviously: "There's a fellow who saves an awful lot of money!" (GILIAN's *tinkling laugh*; SEYMOUR *smiles*) But have you noticed—well, I suppose you children are too young to notice . . .

GILIAN Thank you, Brock dear. It's the only nice thing you've ever said to me!

BROCK Compared to me you *are* children. No one who is not, as I am, over seventy knows what it is to be over seventy. This morning, coming back from the church, I felt an extraordinary excitement, an extraordinary joy in living. I relished each instant and the miracles it contained: the sights from the cab—the fact that I was able to see the back of the cabbie's neck—it all became cherishable. The vastness, the intricacy, the cunning contradictions of sheer consciousness—at my disposal, denied to Clyde. That it was withheld forever from Clyde intensified my sense of well-being. Rather awful, isn't it?

GILIAN Naturally!

BROCK (*Tolerantly*) Don't reverse our roles, Gilian. I am the one who insults *you*!

GILIAN Do your worst tonight. I am so armored in happiness that nothing you can say will affect me in the least.

BROCK If you are happy, dear one, some victim must be in pain.

GILIAN (*To* SEYMOUR) Are you in pain, Seymour?

BROCK (*Very quick—to* SEYMOUR) Before you entangle yourself with Gilian, Seymour, you'd better talk to *me*.
(CHARLIE *comes back*)

CHARLIE Oh, Brock! Hello!
(BROCK *salutes him, military-style*)

GILIAN (*To* CHARLIE) Is Doctor Greer coming?

CHARLIE He's going to try.

BROCK (*To* CHARLIE) You're his patient aren't you, Charlie? Does he help you?

CHARLIE I help *him*!

GILIAN By getting him patients like Seymour. (*To* SEYMOUR) Don't go, Seymour. I'll do more for you than he can.

SEYMOUR (*To* GILIAN) Have you been analyzed?

119

GILIAN Only by myself. And not too closely, at that! I hate being over-explained. I don't want to know *why* I do anything. I just enjoy doing it.

BROCK For once I agree with you, Gilian. Has anyone tried to analyze Iago? I think he would have resisted it!

GILIAN (*Pleased*) What makes you think of Iago in connection with me?

BROCK Free association. They're always rooting, these psychiatrists, for antecedent causes for evil conduct. I don't think there was any antecedent cause for Iago. He was just naturally mean. This search for motives behind bad actions seems to me silly. It is based on the assumption that people are naturally good. It is an untested assumption. The history of the inhuman race contradicts it. Maybe people are just naturally bad. It is virtue that should be explained. That's where the hidden motive should be sought.

(HARRY *comes in, excited and beaming*)

HARRY The violist is here! We can start!

SEYMOUR Can't we wait a few minutes—for Faith and Willard?

HARRY Oh, they're up there. They went straight up to your place in the elevator.

(GILIAN *gets up*, BROCK *remains seated*)

GILIAN Come on, Brock. You'll absorb culture.

BROCK (*Pitifully*) Do I have to go up? Can't I listen from here? I love this room—this chair—this bar.

HARRY (*Shocked*) But, Mr. Dunnaway! Don't you love chamber music?

BROCK Not in the least.

HARRY (*Hurt, appalled, he appeals to all of them solemnly*)
But in chamber music the composers expressed all their
most intimate thoughts.

BROCK But you forget, dear Harry, I have intimate
thoughts of my own and they bore the hell out of me.
Now why should I be interested in the intimate thoughts
of dead composers?

HARRY (*Shaking his head*) He shouldn't say things like
that—even as a joke!
(HARRY *goes out.* BROCK *gets up*)

SEYMOUR (*Joins him, starts to walk him out*) There's a
bar in my place too, you know, Brock.
(*He walks* BROCK *out of the room*)

BROCK (*Goes but protesting*) It would have been so
pleasant just to sit here and talk. I knew this house
when I first came to New York. It was occupied by a
shipping tycoon and his lovely wife. She was my first
love. She was so lovely—and so indiscreet . . .
(BROCK *and* SEYMOUR *go out,* GILIAN *and* CHARLIE
following. As the latter reach the door, CHARLIE
stops a minute)

CHARLIE Well, Gilian?

GILIAN Well?

CHARLIE Still going to Stockholm?

GILIAN (*Winds her arm through his affectionately*)
Didn't I tell you, darling, not to underestimate me?
(*As they go out the lights dim*)

Scene Two

Scene: The same. A half-hour later. Through the open door and during a good part of the following scene, we hear the exquisite melody of the slow movement of the Schubert A-Minor Quartet.

At rise: GILIAN *walks in, followed by* WILLARD. WILLARD *wears the same shabby suit he wore in Act One.*

GILIAN (*As she walks in and goes to her accustomed chair*) Leave the door open, will you, darling? (*As she sits and the music comes through*) Isn't it exquisite? To listen from here without having to look at the faces of the players? Those faces are not quite ethereal, are they? Those jowls pressed on the shells of the instruments. I feel every moment they'll break. So *distracting!* I'm on champagne tonight. Get me some, there's a dear boy. (WILLARD *goes to the bar, pours some champagne, brings it to her. She looks up at him*) How do you feel?

WILLARD Light as air. Free as air. Liberated, marvelous.

GILIAN Liberated from what?

WILLARD From myself.

GILIAN That's meaningless. You can't be liberated from yourself. Why should you want to be? Whatever you are—you are. You're stuck with it!

WILLARD (*Smiles*) Perhaps, I meant, liberated from you.

GILIAN I don't believe that either. The moment I caught your eye—up there—you knew that I wanted to get out of there, didn't you? And you got up to go before I did. Your father and I were like that. We knew, without speaking, what the other was thinking. (WILLARD *kneels beside her, caresses her face*) Your father used to make that gesture. He worshiped me, you know. When he was sober.

WILLARD   I am not sober. And I worship you.

GILIAN   Sweet! You're sweet tonight.

WILLARD   I no longer hope for anything from you. I no longer want anything from you . . .

GILIAN   When did that happen?

WILLARD   Just now. Upstairs. Listening to the music.

GILIAN   It's just as well. We bother everybody, you know. We worry everybody. And, as the President says in his press conferences, "I have an announcement to make."

WILLARD   What?

GILIAN   I intend to marry Seymour.

WILLARD   My blessing!

GILIAN   Is that all?

WILLARD   I am too poor to give you anything else.

GILIAN   I'll be influential, won't I? I'll see that Seymour gives you that grant.

WILLARD   I don't want the grant.

GILIAN   That's perverse. Why not?

WILLARD I am going to follow the example of a friend of mine—and become a Trappist monk. (*She laughs*) I'm sick of the sound of my own voice. It'll be heaven— no longer to have to listen to it.

GILIAN I love your voice. It's a charming voice. It's your father's voice.

WILLARD I love your face. And yet—when I look at it— I see my dead brother's face.

GILIAN I know you blame me for that. So unjust. But then, Willard—we have to face it—you're psychotic, aren't you, as your father was? (*A pause. The music comes through clearly. Finally*) Was the world really as harmonious and as tranquil as that, do you think, when Schubert wrote it? Or was it a lie? Were they all jangled up just as we are only they didn't have the courage to admit it? What do you think? Art was like a formal garden, wasn't it, in those days?

WILLARD Those six weeks when I was in prison . . .

GILIAN Yes?

WILLARD I wrote a quite lovely lyric. I did it to get away from my thoughts.

GILIAN What were your thoughts?

WILLARD Hatred of my father. And not on account of my dead brother. No. That's not accurate. It wasn't hatred. It was jealousy. I remembered how you kissed me and I was jealous. I was jealous of his success, of his greatness. Because it was that success and that greatness that gave him you.

GILIAN (*She is caressing his hair—she is titillated by this*) Poor boy! *Were* you jealous? Were you?

WILLARD   And yet my lyric reflected none of that. Nothing of what I was feeling. It was about birds in flight.

GILIAN   The formal garden!

WILLARD   Yes.

GILIAN   I have been—all this time—on the verge with you.

WILLARD   I no longer care.

GILIAN   (*Her hand still caressing his hair*)   That's not gallant.

WILLARD   Shall I lie to you?

GILIAN   I am tempted to give in. My last fling. Before I settle down with Seymour. (*He kneels by her side, holding her hand. He kisses her hands*) Your father always felt a sense of guilt. Will you feel a sense of guilt?

WILLARD   Be careful, darling.

GILIAN   I'm not in the least afraid of you. Or—if I am— I enjoy it. Life is monotonous. I enjoy the whiff of danger.

WILLARD   I have often wished to kill you.

GILIAN   I know.

WILLARD   At the same time . . .

GILIAN   I know that too.

WILLARD   I have thought it through. It's not you I want to kill. It's myself I want to kill.

GILIAN Why aren't you more direct—like your father? (WILLARD *laughs. She laughs too. He lies flat on the floor, beside her chair, his hands behind his neck*)

WILLARD You're so logical. It's beautiful—like a formula in mathematics.

GILIAN (*Caressingly*) You are so very gifted. Why haven't you done more? You have your father's gift. Why haven't you imitated him?

WILLARD But my father wasn't inhibited and I am.

GILIAN Don't be inhibited. There's no percentage in it.

WILLARD (*After a moment—lazily*) Be careful, Gilian . . .

GILIAN Of what?

WILLARD Of getting involved with me.

GILIAN But I am involved with you.

WILLARD I worship you. Ever since you kissed me that day—I've worshiped you. Was it kindness made you do it?

GILIAN I don't think so.

WILLARD What was it then?

GILIAN I wanted to.

WILLARD But you haven't really wanted to since? (GILIAN *says nothing. He insists*) Have you?

GILIAN You'll find out—one of these days.

126

WILLARD I'll never find out because I am never going to see you again.

GILIAN Really?

WILLARD Really. I am going away.

GILIAN Where?

WILLARD (*Smiles charmingly up at her*) None of your God-damn business.

GILIAN In that case—you may find out before. You may find out now.

WILLARD I warn you, Gilian. You know, we psychotics are very cunning.

GILIAN I wasn't afraid of your father. Do you think I'll be afraid of you?

WILLARD (*Humorously*) Remember I warned you!
  (BROCK *comes in. Sees* WILLARD *lying on the floor*)

BROCK Ah! The Beatnik Recumbent! But I interrupt.

GILIAN Not at all. In fact—your entrance is timely.
  (*She gets up, walks toward him.* WILLARD *gets up too.* BROCK *sits in* GILIAN'*s chair*)

BROCK (*To* WILLARD) I hear you've been tapped for Skull and Bones, Willard. You're put out to pasture with me on Seymour's money. Did I tell you by the way that I enjoyed your book—what there is of it—enormously? I do hope you'll have sense enough not to finish it. It can't possibly sell—it's too subtle and too well written. Do as I am doing—keep getting extensions from the Foundation. (*He sits*) God, that music bored me. And

127

the devotional expression of the listeners! They think just because they're listening to music that they're doing something elevated. We're living in a wonderful time, Willard. When I was young there were no Guggenheims, no Fulbrights, no Rosenthals. We became expert in the technique of eating without food.

GILIAN (*Cuts through this*) Brock—

BROCK Yes, asp.

GILIAN You can do me a favor as recompense for all the compliments you've paid me over the years.

BROCK If I can do it without getting up, I'll do it.

GILIAN If anyone comes in—if anyone asks for us—say that Willard and I have gone for a ride in the Park in a hansom, will you?
(WILLARD *is watching her narrowly*)

BROCK I will.

GILIAN Do you promise?

BROCK I promise. I love little chores like that.
(*Without a word* GILIAN *turns and walks into the bedroom. A moment.* WILLARD *and* BROCK *exchange a look.* WILLARD's *expression has changed—it is very tense.* BROCK *grins at him*)

BROCK At my age I can no longer act. I can only observe.
(*Swiftly* WILLARD *follows* GILIAN *into the bedroom, shutting the door after him. There is the sound of the key turning in the lock.* BROCK *sits for a moment looking at the locked door. He grins, happy as a*

Cheshire cat: the episode gives him enormous pleasure. The hall door is open; the music comes in strongly now that there is silence in the room. BROCK *gets up, goes to the bar, mixes himself a highball. As he returns with the drink to his chair, almost audibly purring,* FAITH *comes in. She wears a charming, simple evening frock. She is disturbed)*

BROCK   Oh, Faith, come in. Do Schubert's most intimate thoughts bore you too?

FAITH   No. I love it. It's beautiful.

BROCK   Why, then, do you absent yourself from felicity?

FAITH   Where's Willard? Have you seen him?

BROCK   He was just in here—talking to me.

FAITH   I saw him walk out with Gilian.

BROCK   They were both here. Just a minute ago.

FAITH   Where are they?

BROCK   Gilian had an impulse to take a turn in the Park in a hansom. She felt stuffy in here.

FAITH   Did they say when they'd be back?

BROCK   Not a word.

FAITH   Was Willard all right?

BROCK   Seemed as happy as a Princeton boy whose sweetheart has just told him he could take her to the Senior Prom.

129

FAITH (*She is lingering at the door*)   If you see him before I do—tell him to come up, will you? It was rather rude of them, I think, to walk out like that.

BROCK   They were listening from here. They got tired of listening from here. Stay and talk to me, Faith.

FAITH   I want to get back to the music.

BROCK   Why?

FAITH   Because I love it.

BROCK   Don't be hypocritical.

FAITH (*Laughs*)   You're hopeless, Brock!

BROCK   Of course I am. What else can you be at my age? The most you can achieve is a kind of damp independence. But I have had an interesting past. Don't you want to hear some delicious anecdotes from my throbbing past?

FAITH   I'd love to but not now. Harry'll be hurt if he sees I'm not there.
> (FAITH *goes out.* BROCK, *full of contentment, sits, sipping his highball. His eye wanders to the bedroom door*)

BROCK (*Aloud to himself—his voice sharp with irony*) Ah! Youth! Youth!
> (*The lights dim down, not to a complete blackout but simply to indicate passage of time. When they go up again* BROCK *is at the bar, refilling his highball glass.* CHARLIE *comes in*)

BROCK   Hello, Maestro! Delighted to see you! (*He walks back to his chair with his drink*) Arnold Bennett once said to me—you know he was fascinated by hotels—

CHARLIE   Those God-damn musicians are inexhaustible. Every time I think, "Ah! They've reached the end," they start in all over again.

BROCK   (*Inexorable, once he starts a story he must finish it*) He was a dear man, Bennett, and as I say, he was fascinated by hotels. His real ambition, he once told me, was to run a really first-class hotel. Because, he said, if you run a really first-class hotel, you don't have to seek out anybody. Everybody who is anybody will eventually come to you. That is the way it is with me in this room. I sit here. Everybody comes to me. (CHARLIE *starts toward the bedroom door*) Charlie . . .

CHARLIE   (*Stops*)   What?

BROCK   Faith was just in here. She said it was rude of me to leave when the musicians are giving their all. Perhaps it is. Let's go back.

CHARLIE   Have you seen Gilian?

BROCK   She was just in here.

CHARLIE   With Willard?

BROCK   With Willard.

CHARLIE   Where are they then?

BROCK   They went for a ride in the Park in a hansom. Juvenile, isn't it?

CHARLIE   (*Incredulous*)   In a hansom!

131

BROCK   Yes. You've seen them. For nostalgics.

CHARLIE   In the Park!

BROCK   Yes. You've seen *it*. The Eden of juvenile delinquents. They carve you up so nicely there.
(CHARLIE *comes close to* BROCK—*looks at him*)

CHARLIE   Something tells me that you are a God-damn liar!
(*At this moment there is the sound through the bedroom door of a scuffle, a sharp cry, a heavy blow and the thud of a falling body.* BROCK *holds onto* CHARLIE's *arm in a tight grip so he can't move*)

BROCK   (*In a kind of ecstasy*)   May the best man win!
(CHARLIE *tries to tear his arm loose, but* BROCK *is strong and tenacious*)

CHARLIE   I knew you were lying!
(*He tries to shake his arm free*)

BROCK   Why expose yourself, unnecessarily, on the line of fire?
(*But* CHARLIE *succeeds. He starts toward the door in a fury*)

BROCK   In any case, the door is locked.
(CHARLIE *reaches the door, tries it and then starts banging on it. Inside there is silence now*)

CHARLIE   Gilian—open the door—it's my room! Open the door!
(*He keeps banging maniacally at the door—it suddenly opens*)

GILIAN (*Over her shoulder—into the room*) Lie there, scum!

(CHARLIE *rushes past her into the room*)

GILIAN (*To* BROCK) Brock—a brandy please. (BROCK *jumps to obey.* GILIAN—*feeling her throat—leans back against the bedroom door. She is terribly shaken but also triumphant.* BROCK *comes to her with a brandy glass.* GILIAN *takes it*) Thank you. I've telephoned the police. Isn't it funny? I'm always having to arrest Willard. (*She lifts her glass to him*) Cheers!

(*She gulps the brandy—*BROCK *stares at her. A moment.* GILIAN *pulls herself together—starts for the stairs, her hand still on her neck*)

GILIAN (*As she passes* BROCK) Brock—am I presentable?

BROCK Passably.

GILIAN (*As she starts up the stairs*) I need a tranquilizer. Franz Schubert beckons me!

(*As* BROCK *looks after her—titillated and admiring —the lights black out*)

Scene Three

Scene: The same. Late afternoon, a few days later.

At rise: SEYMOUR *is at the desk. He has a sheet of paper before him on which a poem is written. It affects him. He puts the poem down. He leans over the table, his hands over his eyes.* CHARLIE *comes in.*

CHARLIE   What's the matter?

SEYMOUR (*Comes to*)   Oh, nothing . . . I was just reading those poems again . . . that young Irish girl . . .

CHARLIE   Sheila Maloney's?

SEYMOUR   Yes. I've asked her to come in. Know anything about her?

CHARLIE   It's hard to get anything out of her. Very withdrawn—poverty-stricken—scared.

SEYMOUR   Charlie . . .

CHARLIE (*Looks at him*)   You look done in.

SEYMOUR   Do I?

CHARLIE   What's wrong?

SEYMOUR   I'm worried, Charlie.
(*He gets up, starts to pace the room*)

CHARLIE (*Trying to sound unconcerned*)   Maybe that trip to Stockholm with Gilian—will rest you.

SEYMOUR (*After a moment*)   I am terribly troubled, Charlie. About many things—

134

CHARLIE (*Wary*) For instance?

SEYMOUR This difference between us—over Willard . . .

CHARLIE Surely that is settled now!

SEYMOUR How do you mean—settled?

CHARLIE Surely there could be no question of giving him a grant *now*?

SEYMOUR Now, I should think, more than ever.

CHARLIE (*In protest*) You can't be serious. He's a homicidal maniac in custody in Bellevue, where he belongs.

SEYMOUR (*He passes his hand over his eyes in weariness*) It seems very strange to me . . .

CHARLIE (*His temper beginning to rise*) What?

SEYMOUR Gilian is perfectly well. She hit Willard with a paperweight so hard that he has a concussion of the brain. And yet Willard is in custody.

CHARLIE (*Very angry*) Now really, Seymour! You don't make sense. Willard was going to strangle her. If Gilian hadn't been—resourceful—she'd be dead now and Willard would be up for murder. Would you still want to give him the grant?

SEYMOUR (*In pain, but with an indomitable clarity and conviction; he is very quiet*) Do you know what happened in that room—what really happened?

CHARLIE Of course I do.

SEYMOUR You know what Gilian told you. You have only heard one side of it.

CHARLIE My God, Seymour, what is this God-damn obsession you seem to have about Willard? Are you in love with him?

SEYMOUR (*Very quiet, very firm*) Don't lose your temper, Charlie. Sit down. (CHARLIE *glares at him; his nerves are frayed*) Please, Charlie. Sit down.
  (CHARLIE *sits*)

CHARLIE Well?

SEYMOUR The other day—when we were discussing this —you brought it up against Willard that he didn't like you. That he had made contemptuous remarks about me, about the Foundation.

CHARLIE So he did.

SEYMOUR You were prepared to turn him down then— on personal grounds?

CHARLIE I was prepared to turn him down because I knew he was a hysteric and a drunk and irresponsible. And now he has so conveniently justified all my fears.

SEYMOUR You told Faith I had turned Willard down— when I hadn't. You reproached Faith for sending the book to me. Going over your head, you called it. Isn't that a petty consideration—a petty vanity—when you consider what was in balance—a human life, perhaps— certainly a talent . . .

CHARLIE We decided at the beginning that authority was to rest in me . . .

SEYMOUR I believed you would exercise it—justly.

CHARLIE You are sentimental—just as you were with Brock . . .

SEYMOUR There is an inch of conflict here—an inch. I suppose, in the welter in which we live, trivial and unimportant. Still, this tiny issue . . .

CHARLIE (*Truculent*) Well?

SEYMOUR This inch over which you had control involves a question of responsibility. I hate to say it, Charlie— I have to steel myself to say it—but, in my view, you have proved yourself irresponsible.

CHARLIE Did I hear you correctly? Did you say—"had" control?

SEYMOUR Yes.

CHARLIE What does that mean exactly?

SEYMOUR I have come to a decision, Charlie.

CHARLIE Well?

SEYMOUR I have decided to run the Foundation myself. I want to devote all my time to it.
(*A pause.* CHARLIE *looks at him without moving*)

CHARLIE (*Finally*) You're firing me.

SEYMOUR (*Very quiet*) I want you to resign. As I say, Charlie—you are too personal. I want this Foundation to be run—impersonally. I want it to consider, in its applicants, only two things: merit and need.

CHARLIE Including criminals?

137

SEYMOUR (*Dryly*) Dear Charlie. You can't impose a strict moral code on artists. But I think you must on executives. If an executive—at least in an enterprise like this—hasn't got that—what *has* he got?

CHARLIE I'll be God damned!

SEYMOUR You must know, dear Charlie, that this isn't easy for me.

CHARLIE You're not saying these things to me. I'm dreaming.

SEYMOUR I don't have to say—do I?—that on the financial side—

CHARLIE (*Bitter—walks toward* SEYMOUR *with drink*) Severance pay!

SEYMOUR I knew it would be difficult. You are making it more difficult. But I will say what I have to say. On the financial side I will be generous. You'll have no worry on that score. And also—before you call my attention to it—I will tell you that I haven't forgotten the past. I remember everything, how you befriended me at Yale, how generous you were, how you stood by me when I was alone and swamped in a sense of inadequacy. I know all that. I remember all that. But, also, I have allowed my sense of gratitude to obscure my vision of you. I am slow. I am very slow.

CHARLIE (*Thinking fast, quietly*) All right. Give Willard the grant. It's O.K. with me.

SEYMOUR But Charlie! It is not O.K. with you. Why do you say it is?

138

CHARLIE (*With mounting anger*) Because while you have always been so generous and gallant as to say that I, and not you, was the boss, it has obviously been all along a fiction. I don't know why you choose this moment to assert the reality. Well, let's face the reality. Let's proceed henceforth on the basis of reality. I'll make the recommendations—you accept or veto them. When you make them—that will be that. We're grown men. We're old friends. Does it have to dissolve, this friendship, on a difference of opinion in one bizarre instance?

SEYMOUR Yes. It does.

CHARLIE In the name of good sense—will you tell me why?

SEYMOUR Your willingness now—to yield on this issue—merely illustrates what I mean. I don't want obedience. I want conviction. It's awfully difficult for me to say these things—without sounding—holier-than-thou . . .

CHARLIE (*Decides to re-animate his well-known charm*) When you're holier-than-thou with *me*, you're giving yourself a wide margin!

SEYMOUR (*Smiles*) I do hope I won't lose you—as a friend. You are so very amusing. You are so frank about yourself.

CHARLIE (*Keeping it up*) That's my pose—frankness.

SEYMOUR That is amusing too. But I don't want the Foundation run by a man with whom frankness is a pose. The time is too—exacting . . .

CHARLIE Oh, I'm tired of hearing that. This time's no different from any other time. There were always wars

139

and troubles. What difference does it make to the corpse if he's killed by a bow and arrow—a howitzer—or an atomic bomb? There were always those who went under —and those who survived. You're blowing up this thing out of all proportion.

SEYMOUR   It is particularly necessary—in a time like this —to be scrupulous.

CHARLIE   Are you suggesting that I am *un*scrupulous?

SEYMOUR   It's a matter of simple justice.

CHARLIE   Who the hell is just? Who can be?

SEYMOUR   No one can be. But you can at least know when you're not.
(*A pause. Somehow, now* CHARLIE *realizes the jig is up. He gets up in a terrible fury; loses all control of himself*)

CHARLIE (*Faces* SEYMOUR *with outright hostility*)   You're pretty clever! You're pretty cunning. You do pretty well for yourself, don't you? Are you showing off in front of Gilian? Is that it? Now that you're going to marry Gilian you want to show her you don't depend on me? It's about the only way you can show Gilian that you are strong, virile! By firing your oldest friend. Well, all I can say is, that I hope this display will satisfy her, on the boat to Stockholm!

SEYMOUR (*Stutters a bit*)   You see, Charlie. You're— *personal!*

CHARLIE   What the hell do you expect me to be? You snitched Gilian away from me. And not as a man may take a woman away from another man. By drafts of holier-than-thou's made out to cash! When I think of those early years, when you used to come whimpering to me like a spaniel . . .

(GILIAN *walks in*)

GILIAN   Hello, boys! (*Neither of them says anything*) What's the matter? Lovers' quarrel? Over me, I hope!

CHARLIE (*With hatred, to* SEYMOUR)   I can't bear the sight of either of you! (*He starts for the door to his room*) I hope I may still have the use of this apartment —for a few days at least!

(*He goes blindly into his room and slams the door*)

GILIAN (*Astonished*)   What on earth's gotten into Charlie . . . ? Is it about me?

SEYMOUR (*Shaken but quiet*)   Partly.

GILIAN   Don't give it a thought, darling. I'll scold him about it. He'll be as sweet as honey, I promise you. He'll come to see us off.

SEYMOUR   I'm not going.

GILIAN (*A moment*)   Why not?

SEYMOUR   No point in telling you the reasons.

GILIAN   But this isn't like you. You told me you were going. You don't lie! It is one of your eccentricities which I find so appealing.

SEYMOUR   You said something the other day . . . it's odd, Gilian . . . while you were saying it I wasn't really listening . . . but then afterward I heard you saying it . . .

141

GILIAN (*Sympathetically*) You *after-heard* it?

SEYMOUR Yes.

GILIAN That often happens to me. What did I say?

SEYMOUR You spoke of my "good works"—so you called them—and said you didn't believe in them, but that you would permit me to indulge them . . .

GILIAN (*Kindly*) Oh, but, darling, surely you haven't changed your mind on account of those idle words. Where's your sense of humor?

SEYMOUR I am not sure I have a sense of humor.

GILIAN You must have a sense of humor or I wouldn't adore you as I do. Craig hadn't a grain. He told clumsy jokes at which he laughed appreciatively, but he had no humor.

SEYMOUR It isn't what you said—the words you said—it was the *tone*. The tone of all of you. You are all so amusing! It is really too cynical—too unfeeling—I don't really belong, you know.

GILIAN You don't have to belong. I am sophisticated enough for both of us. Now tell me really why you're not going to Stockholm. Why did you say you'd go?

SEYMOUR Because I thought it would break it up—between you and Willard.

GILIAN (*A moment*) As an assist to Faith?

SEYMOUR You might put it that way.

GILIAN Are you in love with Faith?

142

SEYMOUR   Yes.

GILIAN   What stops you?

SEYMOUR   For one thing—she doesn't know it.

GILIAN   Why don't you inform her?

SEYMOUR   (*Turns away*)   Don't pump me, Gilian, please.

CILIAN   The amusing thing is—it would have worked. I wasn't going to see Willard any more. But there he was —that night. Are you sure—that Stockholm is off?

SEYMOUR   Stockholm is off.

GILIAN   (*Smiles*)   Shall I work on you?

SEYMOUR   Please don't. Nothing could induce me to go.

GILIAN   (*Musing aloud, struck by the incredible wonder of it*)   Imagine! My losing a man to that little Faith Prosper!
   (FAITH *comes in. She freezes at the sight of* GILIAN)

SEYMOUR   How's Willard?

FAITH   He's going to be all right, thank God.

GILIAN   I have instructed my lawyer—not to prefer charges against Willard. Seymour . . . do you mind if I go in to see Charlie for a minute?

SEYMOUR   Not at all.

GILIAN   (*As she moves toward the door, then stops when she gets there; to* FAITH)   When you see Willard again —give him my love. I bear no grudges. I'm not vindictive, you see.
   (*She goes out*)

SEYMOUR   I am glad to hear—that Willard is out of the woods.

FAITH   When I left the hospital just now I walked into a church and knelt and prayed and thanked God.

SEYMOUR   I wish you'd bring me to see him.

FAITH   It would be wonderful if you would.

SEYMOUR   If he's in the mood to discuss it—I'd like to talk to Willard—about his book . . .

FAITH   (*A bit incredulous*)   You mean—nothing is changed about that?

SEYMOUR   Why should it be?
    (FAITH *turns away, overcome*)

FAITH   I am always breaking down with you! Damn it! I love you, Seymour.

SEYMOUR   (*Thinks perhaps this is the moment to inform her*)   I love you, Faith.

FAITH   And I came here to tell you . . .
    (*She turns, in control of herself, comes to him*)

SEYMOUR   Yes?

FAITH   You are my dearest friend. You are the dearest friend I have in the world. And therefore I want to tell you . . . I am going to marry Harry. I want your blessing. *We* want your blessing.

SEYMOUR   You have my blessing.

FAITH   He is a dear man. When you get to know him— you'll see—what a dear man he is. Willard is very happy about it. He was afraid, you know, that I was going to marry Charlie. I see now that there was never any real danger—thanks to Charlie—but Willard didn't know that. And for a long time—neither did I.

SEYMOUR   I think you have chosen wisely. I do.

FAITH   We'll have good times. We'll have music parties. And you'll come.

SEYMOUR (*Smiles at her*)   I will certainly come.

FAITH   I am so lucky. To have Willard. To have Harry. To have you.
(*Impulsively she flings her arms around him and kisses him.* GILIAN *comes in*)

GILIAN (*As* FAITH *breaks away*)   Ah, Seymour. I see you took my suggestion. You *did* inform her. (*To* FAITH) Congratulations, Faith!

FAITH (*Breathless*)   Thank you. But how did you know? (*To* SEYMOUR—*under her breath*) I'll arrange it and call you.

SEYMOUR   Do.
(FAITH *runs out*)

GILIAN (*Looks after* FAITH, *in admiration of an exercise in technique*)   Well, very clever that little girl! I always thought her stupid, to tell you the truth. Didn't know she had it in her. Didn't know you had it in *you*. Well, at least one of Craig's children has turned out well!

SEYMOUR (*Soberly*)   Yes. She has turned out very well.

GILIAN Isn't it conceited of you to say so? It's the first time I've ever known you to make an arrogant remark. Good sign! (*Looks at him sharply*) But you don't seem exactly the happy bridegroom. What's the matter? Have you got cold feet?

(CHARLIE *comes in. As he does the telephone rings. He answers it*)

CHARLIE Oh, Alvin, how are you . . . I was just going to call you . . . I have to cancel our date . . . Sailing for Stockholm Wednesday . . . just decided . . . not quite alone . . . Gilian's sailing too. Isn't it a lucky coincidence? Expect you to see us off . . . Expect Seymour to see us off too and maybe you can nab him at the pier . . . Okey-doke.

(*He hangs up—faces* SEYMOUR)

SEYMOUR I'm very pleased for you, Charlie.

GILIAN Never in my life have I been so ignominiously dismissed! Maybe it's the tolling of the bell for me? Is it the beginning of the end? My first defeat. Maybe I should retire from the battle?

CHARLIE (*In high humor, completely restored*) You don't know what battle is yet, Gilian. All those minor skirmishes of ours—nothing! From now on you'll find out what battle really is! Come along. (*To* SEYMOUR) I can't wait to pick up that ticket—before our girl changes her mind! I don't mind in the least, Seymour, understudying you. You know what sometimes happens in the theatre—the understudy gives a better performance than the star!

(CHARLIE *and* GILIAN *start out.* CHARLIE *disappears,* GILIAN *lingers for a moment at the door*)

GILIAN   Oh, Seymour—I almost forgot to tell you. I have a message for you from Anna, my cook. She wants to come to work for you. She loves you.

SEYMOUR   I'd love to have her. Who wouldn't? She's a genius.

GILIAN   I'll tell her. She'll be in seventh heaven. She believes you'll be good for her insomnia. You'll come to see us off, won't you?

SEYMOUR   Of course I will.

GILIAN   To show you how big I am I'll let you bring the bride.

SEYMOUR   (*Smiles*)   All right. I'll ask Faith.
(*Just as she is going,* BROCK *comes in*)

BROCK   Ah! Lucretia! Greetings! (*As he moves past her into the room*) I always thought *The Rape of Lucrece* the most boring of Shakespeare's works. I never read it without a strong feeling that Lucrece *cooperated*—don't you agree?

GILIAN   You are a lecherous old man!

BROCK   Of course I am. Why should the young have it all?

GILIAN   I wish I had known you in your youth.

BROCK   You'd not have been disappointed.

147

GILIAN (*Pointedly*) I wonder!
(*She goes*)

BROCK (*To* SEYMOUR) There is an incredibly beautiful dark young lady waiting for you in the hall, Seymour.

SEYMOUR Oh, that's Sheila Maloney. I'll just see her for a minute and then I'm at your service.

BROCK I thought Charlie broke them in.

SEYMOUR No longer.

BROCK Oh?

SEYMOUR I'll tell you all at dinner, Brock. How did you find Willard?

BROCK Remarkably cheerful. I congratulated him. I told him he was probably unique in the history of jurisprudence—the first man who managed to get arrested in a rape case on a triple divorcée.

SEYMOUR (*Smiles*) But he's all right is he? You think he'll be all right?

BROCK Oh yes. Moreover, I got the feeling—I strongly got the feeling—

SEYMOUR Yes?

BROCK That he's finally paid off the inheritance tax. That the vendetta is liquidated at last—

SEYMOUR Did Willard tell you what really happened?

BROCK He did. After embracing Gilian—isn't that an old-fashioned word? Doesn't that date me? (*Enjoys being slow*) After embracing Gilian, Willard did try to kill

148

her. But, having failed, having, in fact, been nearly killed by her, I believe that the compulsion to revenge is satisfied. I do believe that the ghost of his father is now finally laid—(*He recoils in horror*) Oh, dear! That might be mistaken for a pun—and I abhor puns!

SEYMOUR   Well—let's hope—(*A moment*) Will you ask Miss Maloney to come in. I just want to tell her I like her stuff. Then we'll go to dinner.

BROCK   Right. If I were in *your* position I'd ask Miss Maloney to dinner.
(BROCK *goes.* SEYMOUR, *brooding and restless, walks up to the French windows, pulls the curtains aside and looks out. He comes back as* SHEILA MALONEY, *a lovely dark young Irish girl, comes in.* MISS MALONEY *is in an agony of nervous shyness; her hands tremble.* SEYMOUR *comes to greet her*)

SEYMOUR   I'm Seymour Rosenthal. I am very glad to see you.

SHEILA   Thank you.
(SEYMOUR *goes behind desk, motions her to a chair beside him.* SHEILA *sits*)

SEYMOUR   (*The sheaf of poems is before him—he picks them up*) I've been reading your poems again—as a kind of refresher.

SHEILA   It's very kind of you to take the trouble.
(*He smiles and so does she, faintly*)

SEYMOUR   I have never, I think, felt so strongly, that an applicant should have a grant from this Foundation . . .

SHEILA (*Overcome, stammers*) I—I don't know what to say . . .

SEYMOUR You don't have to say anything, Miss Maloney. You have said everything—and beautifully—(*He taps the manuscript*) here . . .
(*As he leans toward her to discuss the details of the grant*)

Curtain